CW01312344

Eileen Beaumont

RAVENSCAR VILLAGE LIFE
After the Town That Never Was!

Eileen Beaumont

Copyright © Eileen Beaumont - 2016

All rights reserved. No part of this publication may be reproduced, stored in a retrieval system, or transmitted, in any form or by any means, electronic, mechanical, photocopying, recording or otherwise, without the prior permission of the copyright owners and the publisher.

Eileen Beaumont asserts her right to be identified as the author of this work in accordance with the Copyright, Designs and Patents Act 1988.
Whilst the author has tried to contact all copyright holders, if you claim to have received no acknowledgement please contact the publisher and a correction will be made to the next edition.

This edition published in Great Britain in 2016 by
Farthings Publishing
8 Christine House
1 Avenue Victoria
SCARBOROUGH
YO11 2QB
UK

http://www.Farthings-Publishing.com
E-mail: queries@farthings.org.uk

ISBN: 978-1-326-64803-9

August 2016 (t)

ACKNOWLEDGEMENTS

I am especially grateful to the following people who have been willing to share their memories of Ravenscar. This has provided a wealth of material enabling me to write this book:-

Mrs H. Chapman, Mrs Falkingham, T. Fry FRSA (Director, the Fry Estate), M. Garbutt, A. Green, G.P. Gridley, Mrs E.A. Hall, Mrs J. Hodgson, F. James, M. Lester & Mrs C. Lester, O. Lancaster, G. Mollon, E. Morgan, Mrs A. Murray, C. Peel, Mr & Mrs J.G. Prince, D.M. Roberts, Miss L.A. Robinson, A. Robinson, the late J.W. Robinson, the late Miss V.E. Robinson, Mrs M. Sawdon, J. Ward, J. White.

A special thank you must go to my husband Howard Beaumont for his encouragement and support throughout.

Public Libraries: Scarborough Library, Leeds Library, the Whitby Literary and Philosophical Society, Whitby Museum.

Newspapers: The Scarborough Gazette, Scarborough Evening News and Mercury, Yorkshire Post and the Northern Echo.

Photographs and postcards have been taken from my own personal collection. My special thanks must go to the many people, who also contributed images which have complimented my work, including:-

Mrs H. Chapman, Frances Frith collection, M. Garbutt, G.P. Gridley, A. Green (collection), Mrs A. Murray, D.M. Roberts, Mrs M. Sawdon, N.E. Stead, J. White, Northern Echo, Scarborough and District Newspapers Ltd.

Cover photograph and drawings by Howard Beaumont.

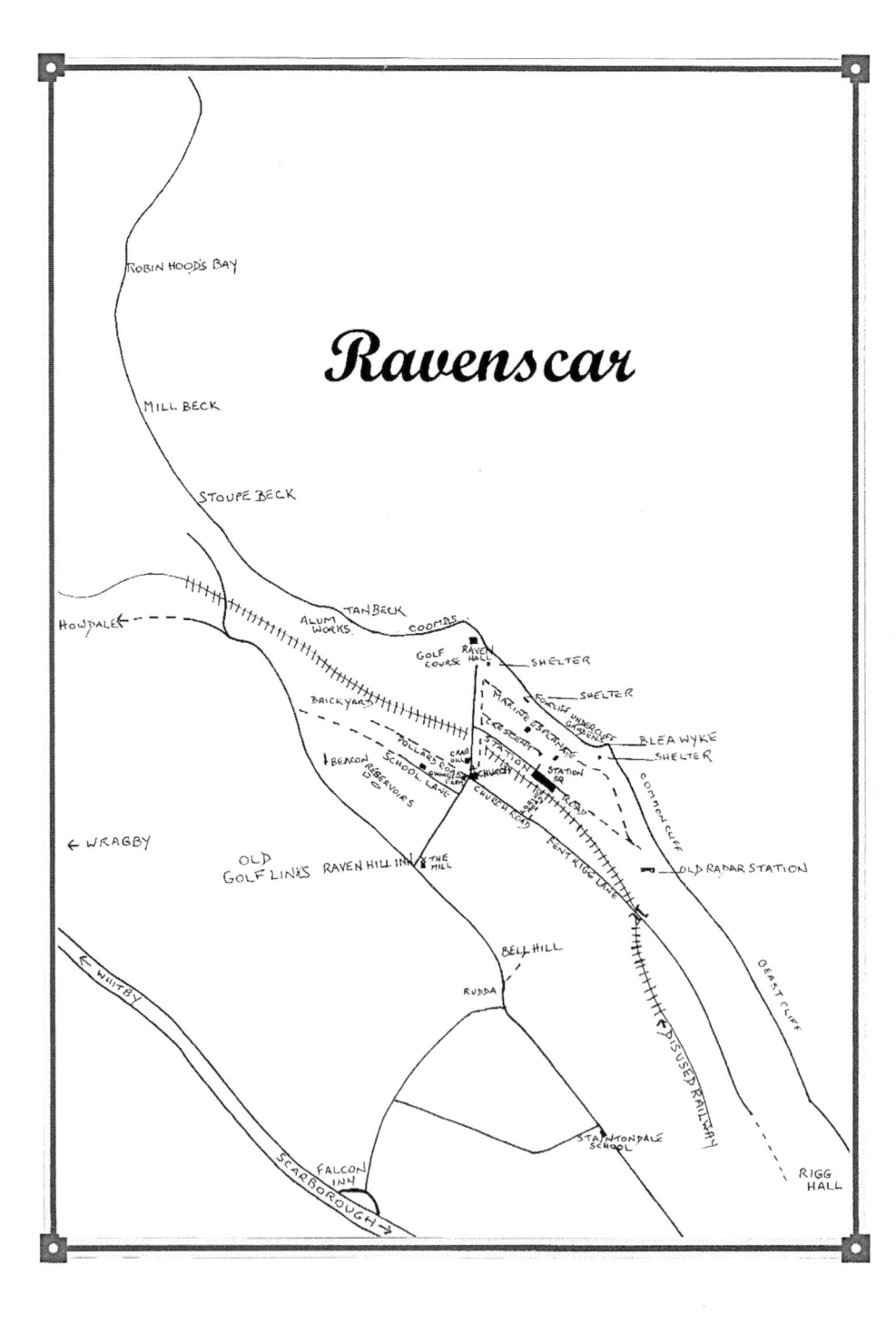

Ravenscar

CONTENTS

	Introduction	9
Chapter 1	Reflections	11
Chapter 2	Expectations	24
Chapter 3	Comings and Goings	39
Chapter 4	Unsettling Times	53
Chapter 5	Normality Returns	70
Chapter 6	The Changing Thirties	91
Chapter 7	Casualties and Heroes	116
Chapter 8	'The Story of my Life'	138
Chapter 9	Hidden Dangers	156
Chapter 10	A Village Forever	181
	Appendix	195

INTRODUCTION

Much has already been documented about Ravenscar, "The Town That Never Was", and the importance of the geology of the surrounding area. Peak House, now known as the Raven Hall Hotel and the Alum Works, have also been researched by several people.

This book covers the social history of a unique village from two decades before the dawn of the twentieth century until the early nineteen eighties and provides a fascinating insight into village life with new revelations and amusing stories from people who lived there during that period.

My grandparents moved to Ravenscar in 1913 as tenant farmers and their descendants lived in the village until 2008. As a result, a mass of information has been passed down from three generations. My Grandmother Robinson lived to receive a telegram from the Queen and two of her surviving daughters at the time of writing are well into their nineties.

The names given to properties can be very confusing; Raven Hill Inn became known as the Blue Robin, then for many years it was called Moorfield House and at that time became a poultry farm, and is now called Smugglers Rock. It is impossible to cover every title change as this could make boring reading. Probably one of the most misleading was in Raven Hall Road. The present Dunholme was called Bay View in 1898, a few years later the detached house two doors away was also given the same name. Finally, Robin Hood Road was always referred to by locals as 'School Lane' following the school being built in 1888.

Over the years there have been several tragic accidents involving locals, however, I have deliberately omitted these in order not to distress any living relatives. In the case of cliff accidents, several involving young people are included. I sincerely hope these occurrences act as a warning for future visitors to take extra care when exploring one of the most imposing stretches of Britain's coastline. After much consideration I have written this book as near as possible in chronological order to make the unfolding story interesting reading.

I hope you take pleasure in having a closer look at a coastal village, which could well have become a seaside resort had the numerous plot sales come to fruition. Thankfully this did not materialise, resulting in a beautiful stretch of Yorkshire coastline being preserved for future generations to enjoy.

***

CHAPTER ONE

REFLECTIONS

On the east coast of Yorkshire six hundred feet above a rocky shoreline, lies the remote village of Ravenscar. This unique hamlet is situated between two well-known historic landmarks: to the north the ruined abbey at Whitby, to the south the Norman keep within the castle walls of the once historic stronghold of Scarborough.

The natural beauty looking across the bay must be one of England's finest sights to behold, with quite an outstanding panorama looking towards the famous fishing village of Robin Hood's Bay. When the calm sea is like a millpond, there is a spectacular phenomenon with the reflections of the buildings and cliffs. In contrast, the inclement weather and the occasional 'bleak mid-winter' with dense fog, high winds, squally showers and wall-high snowdrifts, has given this village an unkindly reputation as a 'draughty hole'. This is also the ideal location to view dazzling sunrises and awesome sunsets, not forgetting the occasional glimpse of the aurora borealis, known as the 'northern lights'. Scattered farmhouses and cottages are strewn haphazardly across the village like chess pieces abandoned in stalemate.

Having set the scene, I now take you the reader, back to the mid-nineteenth century, when Ravenscar was known as Peak. At this time a very productive alum industry, which had flourished for over two hundred years, disappeared, leaving two permanent ugly scars on the landscape. These were the quarries where hard-grafting labourers used picks, shovels and even bare hands to excavate the shale. Others worked in surroundings with the constant stench of stale urine - a vital ingredient for the production of alum. Coal, needed to fuel the boilers, was mined and transported from the Durham pits, then shipped from Hartlepool into a small dock and hauled up the cliff by horse-drawn wagons, or winched on a rail track.

Drawing of the Alum Works

Drawing of the Dock.

After a very complicated process, the finished product was transferred out the same way. Alum had several uses and will probably be best remembered for fixing dye into cloth; but with the invention of synthetic dyes this industry ground to a halt. During the same period jet mining, another local industry, also disappeared in a comparatively short time and all that remains are two mine shaft entrances.

A few years before the closure of the alum industry, a business gentleman from London - W.H. Hammond acquired Peak House. This, the only building of architectural interest, was isolated in a prominent position and enjoyed a commanding view of the bay. In this idyllic location he found his ultimate country retreat and became a benefactor to the village. Mr Hammond decided to build a church in 1852 for the use of all religious denominations. After this time, many Peak Church of England baptism and burial records were entered in parish registers at the nearby village of Cloughton. Shortly after this he was responsible for erecting a windmill that would benefit the whole community. Ground barley was added to pig food and rolled barley became part of the winter fodder for cattle, plus rolled oats gave the horses stamina to do a hard day's work. Finely ground wheat was also important for flour production: just imagine baking days, with homemade crusty-bread served with salty broth from boiled bacon, or even giblets, as a main meal for the poorly paid labourers.

A happy occasion arose when Mr Hammond's second daughter, Henrietta married Thomas William Johnson Barker at the church. The whole village attended the nuptials and this was reported in the Scarborough Mercury on 25th September 1858.

'At an early hour many of the inhabitants of the surrounding neighbourhood assembled to witness the nuptials and to mingle in the gladness of the happy day. The bridal party was escorted to the church by several members of the ancient order of Shepherds attired in their picturesque costume, the Sabbath school children with their banner, the farm and cottage tenantry and the workmen upon the estate.......... and in the evening, music, with a capital display of fireworks,

opposite the Hall, finished the day to the great delight and entertainment of a large number of the inhabitants.'

During the summer of 1863, his daughter Louisa Antoinette married Arthur Marshall of Surrey. In 1883, daughter Emily Jane married John Hill and three years later another daughter, Augusta, married William Henry Bates.

Peak House

Around this time a buzz of excitement circulated throughout the coastal villages between Scarborough and Whitby at the prospects of a rail link. This would provide a faster and more lucrative form of transport, rather than the traditional pony and trap or horse-drawn coaches, and for many - shanks's pony. On July 16th 1885 there was great euphoria when the 'Iron Giants'

W. H. Hammond

arrived at the railway station known as Peak.

Residents were now within easy reach of accessing other villages and towns, rather than having the remoteness of coastal life. The Scarborough Gazette reported on this momentous occasion:

'*The opening of the line for public use to-day, was prefaced yesterday by a social demonstration in honour of the event. A special excursion train ran from Scarborough to Whitby and back, bearing a large party of gentlemen interested in the undertaking, who were invited by the mayor of Scarborough (Robt. Forster, Esq), the directors of Scarborough and Whitby Railway Company, and Messrs. Waddell & Sons, the contractors, to honour the occasion with their presence......*'

The reporter then went on to extol the virtues of the panoramic scene before them, to entice future visitors and holidaymakers to partake of this wonderful amenity:

'*This is another stage at which a halt may well be made and if future excursionists by the line make Peak their destination, they will be abundantly repaid. A glance around reveals the character of the scene. It is full of romantic beauty, wild and magnificent. The bay, which forms the chief feature of the view, is the well-known Robin Hood's Bay. Peak forms what is known as the south cheek of the bay..........*'

However, the village was soon to be shrouded in deep sadness with the passing of its benefactor, Mr Hammond. A report from the Scarborough Gazette of October 29th 1885 states:

'*We regret to announce the death of W.H. Hammond, Esq., of Raven Hall, Peak. He died just before daybreak on Wednesday, the 20th instant, at his home in London, at the advanced age of 83.......... He stirred up the authorities to improve the high roads and make them passable for the average horses and ordinary carriage wheels. He also stirred them up to improve the post, so that Peak was no longer as it had been, six miles away from the nearest delivery of letters. Above all Mr Hammond may be said to have created the Scarborough and Whitby Railway, which now runs through the estate of which his son-in-law, Mr Arthur Marshall is the Chairman. Nearly 20 years ago, he started the idea, obtaining the opinion of eminent engineers............ He was lying in the weakness of approaching death when the new line was opened on the 16th of last July.'*

In the last decade of the nineteenth century, a surprise was looming round the corner which would result in a large upheaval amongst the residents of Peak. By 1896 the estate of the late W.H. Hammond had been sold to a development company. An Abstract of Title of the Ravenscar Estate Limited, registered at Northallerton on the fourteenth of May 1896 Vol.76, refers to '......*the mansion house messuages buildings lands farms hereditaments and premises situate in the Parishes of Staintondale and Fylingdales in the North Riding of the county of York and containing in the whole 637 acres 25 perches or thereabouts.....'.* having been transferred from the trustees Arthur Marshall and William Henry Bates. Legal documents also dated May 1896 from the property known as 'Corbie' showed that Peak Estates Limited was very much up and running. Taken from the Indenture ....*'Two closes or pieces of land and premises forming part of the Hall Farm...... conveyed unto and for the use of the Peak Estate Limited......'*

Great plans were drawn up to convert and build a whole new seaside resort with promenade, shelters, landscaped gardens, and an observatory. This dream development was actively commenced in 1896. An infrastructure of new roads, footpaths, an ambitious drainage system, including water mains from reservoirs, which were fed from a nearby spring, was put in place. There was promise of an abundance of work, but some would have been apprehensive about such a change to their environment. The cliff-top land had a huge variety of wild flowers, birds, bees and butterflies in their natural habitat. This would soon have the appearance of a lattice pie crust: roads crisscrossing from the coastline to the mill, houses sprouting by the dozen supported by at least one hundred shops, along with high hopes of attracting thousands of visitors to four hotels, in addition to the recently converted Raven Hall Hotel.

The negative side of these plans would mean the disappearance of all cattle, horses and sheep grazing the fields. Also missing would be the sight of pigs rooting, accompanied by hens scratching the ground for worms and grubs. From here on, regular auctions selling off the plots of land earmarked for housing, were held at the salerooms adjacent to Raven Hall and in some cases they were only a month apart.

Raven Hall Hotel

Hotel terraced gardens

Not content with building a new town, the directors also changed the name of Peak Estate Limited to that of Ravenscar Estate Limited, which appeared on a certificate dated 14th October 1897 under the hand of the Registrar of Joint Stock Companies. For each sale, a separate map showing the whole area with plot numbers was issued to the relevant buyers.

Having taken a look at life on the land, we should not forget the rugged Yorkshire coastline notorious for shipwrecks caused by the unforgiving North Sea. The bay resembles the jaws of a gigantic whale, with the North Cheek as the upper and the South Cheek as the lower, enticing and capturing prey. Any escaping this hazard could be caught out by the chin at Blea Wyke. Earlier in the same year, tragedy struck during January 1897, when the Londonderry - a Scarborough coal boat owned by Mr Ward, was lost with all hands including his son. It was reported by some sources to have been in distress off Beast Cliff. The Londonderry left Hartlepool for Scarborough on the 21st January. On the 23rd the Scarborough Post reported:

'Last evening a piece of bulwark, with the name 'Londonderry' inserted upon it, was picked up in the vicinity of the Spa wall by a local fisherman.........It is also stated that a ship's ladder had been washed up by the tide and found on the beach near the South Cliff tramway.'

The coast suffered a week of strong northerly winds and blizzards, which probably caused the wreckage to drift ashore several miles south. By the 27th January the Scarborough Post stated: *'All hope of the return of the ill-fated 'Londonderry' has today been abandoned'*.

One Sunday in November 1898, in thick fog, the lower jaw of my imaginary whale snapped up the Umbria, a fishing trawler from Hull. Before the incident she had managed to fill two hundred boxes of fish. On this occasion there was a happy outcome as all eight crew members on board were rescued and taken by lifeboat to Robin Hood's Bay. The trawler, having suffered immense damage, was expected to become a total wreck.

On a lighter side, the same year Ravenscar Golf Club was formed. In 'The History of Yorkshire - Volume 2' originally published in 1912 it states: *'Ravenscar founded on initiative of the Earl of Cranbrooke in 1898, has its 9 hole course 700 ft above the level of the sea, a mile from the coast midway between Whitby and Scarborough'.*

Opening of the Golf Links by the Earl of Cranbrooke August 24th 1898

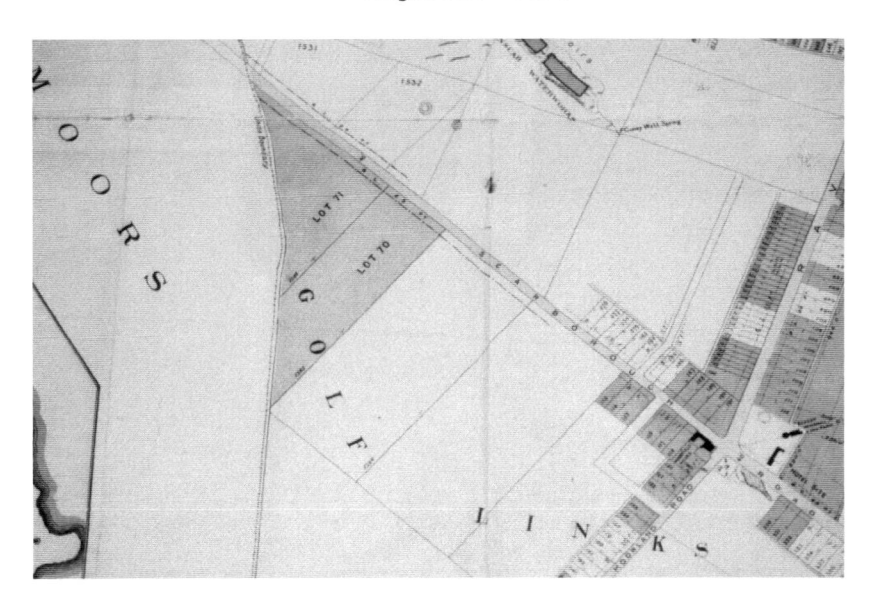

Town Plan showing the golf links

Also by this time the Raven Hall Hotel had been extended to accommodate up to one hundred visitors. The furnishings were carried out by Messrs. Waring of London. It boasted a wine cellar of the highest class and by now was under the management of Hudson Hotels Limited. In the saleroom at the hotel, auctions of plots continued on a regular monthly basis. Special trains ran on the morning of the sale from Bradford, Keighley, and intermediate stations to Leeds to Scarborough, arriving in time to catch the 11.15 am connection to Ravenscar, which prospective Scarborough buyers also boarded. The return train departed at 5.16 pm.

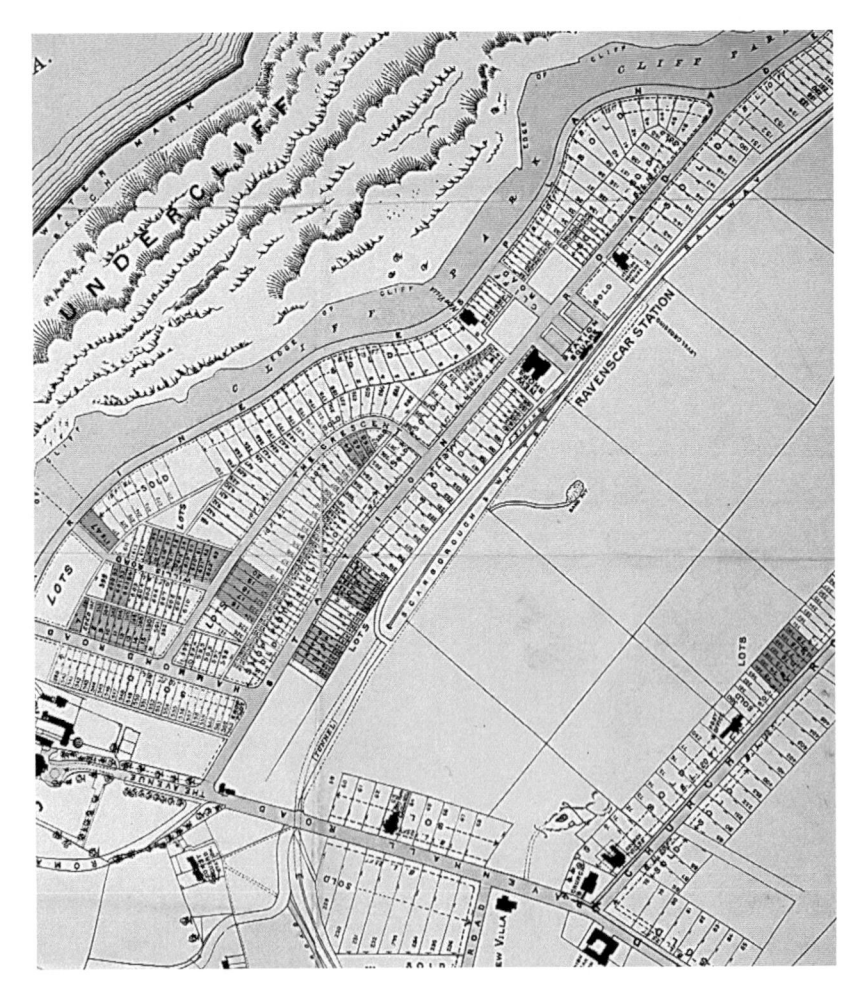

Town Plan, May 1898

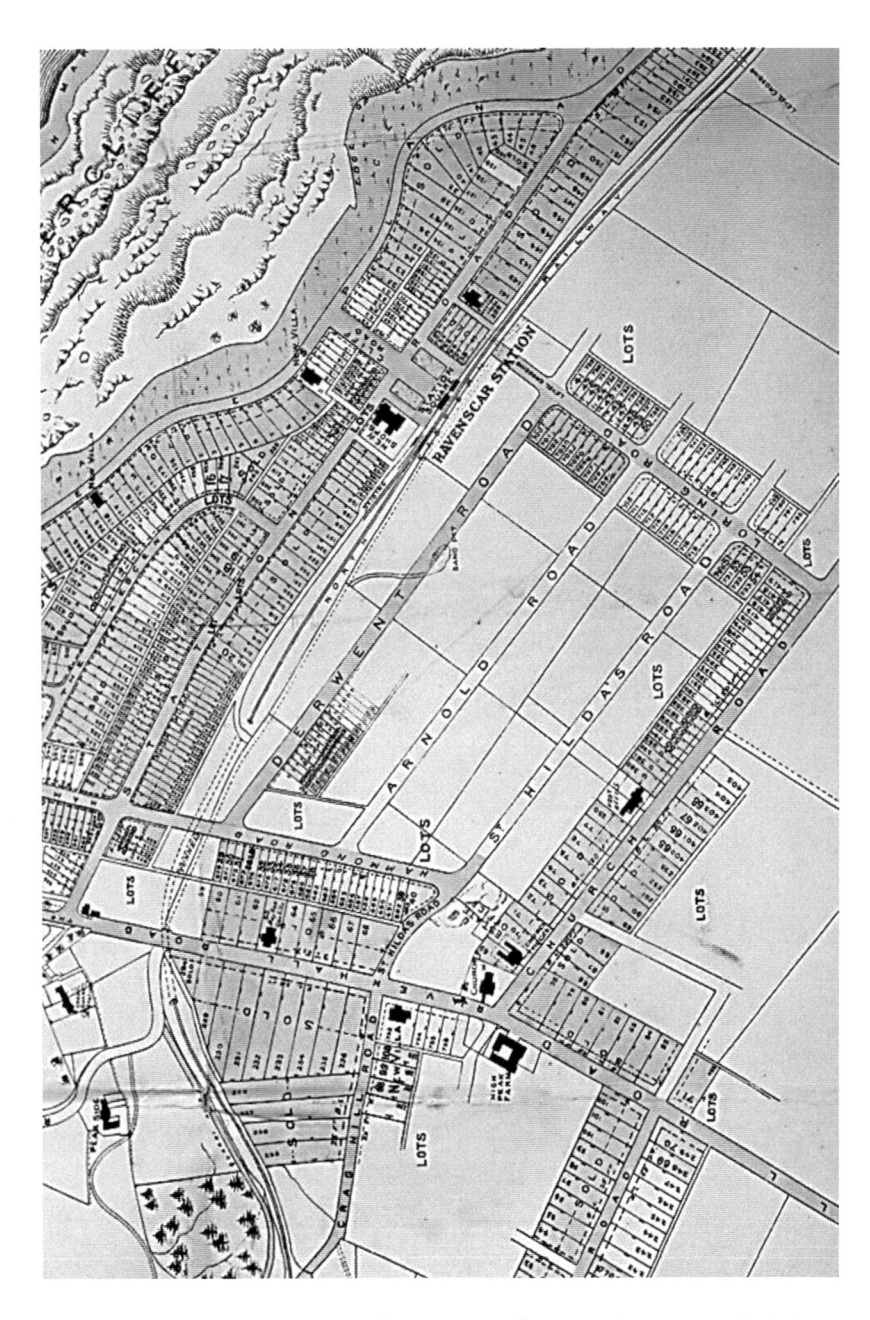

A vast amount of work had been carried out with new roads being finished and plots for sale added in September 1898.

Interestingly, the journey to Leeds was only two hours fifteen minutes. A special offer was extended to prospective clients from the London area: this included return rail-fare from London King's Cross to Ravenscar, with two nights' accommodation at the Royal Hotel Scarborough, all for a tempting price of 20/-. Buyers had their train fares refunded on becoming purchasers. To obtain possession of their building land, a 10% deposit had to be paid. The balance of the purchase money could be paid by instalments over a nine-year period, with interest at 5% per annum. Throughout 1898, the development continued in earnest, and during the summer months Loring Road was constructed. Plot 178 was sold at auction 3 to William Rusby a picture-frame dealer from Leeds: the agreement stated that the property to be built must not be less than £500 in value.

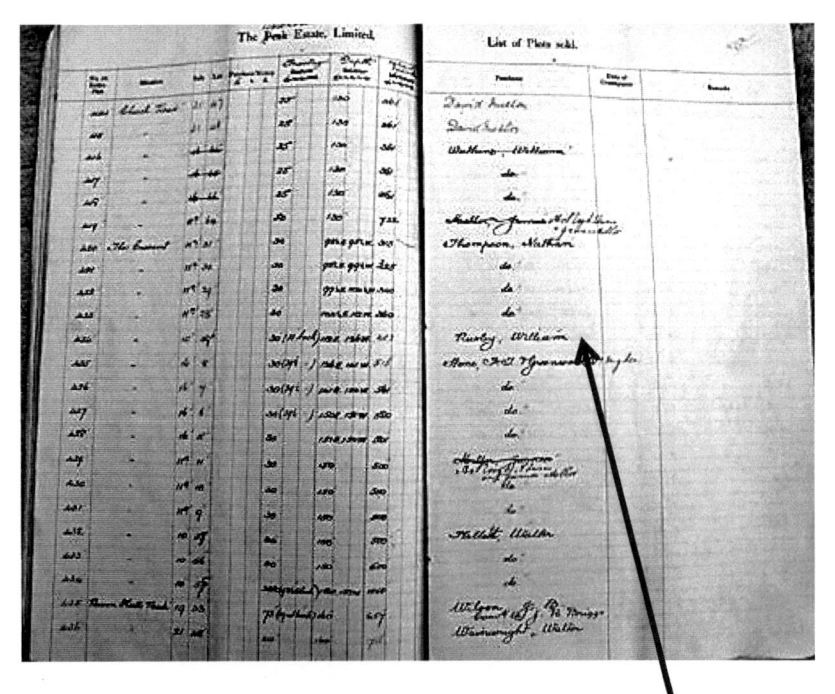

Sales book with Mr Rusby's entry (arrowed)

On June 21st at the tenth sale, he decided to extend his piece of land and bought Lot 59A, plot number 424, on The Crescent. The newly erected 'Sea View Villa' with a large rear garden, stood in an enviable position, with magnificent coastal views. On September 28th Crag Hill Villa in Raven Hall Road was advertised for sale with vacant possession.

'A railway goods siding was opened at the station, which resulted in an important saving in the haulage of building materials. There were immense quarries of stone on the Estate as well as an ample supply of limestone and sand. Excellent brick earth had recently been discovered and experiments in brick-making started.'

As the curtain falls on this century, with the longest-serving monarch, Queen Victoria on the throne and the prospect of this small village becoming a bustling holiday resort, many residents were anticipating what the future might hold.

RAVENSCAR.

AT THE CORNER OF RAVEN HALL & CRAG HILL ROADS.

LOT 42   A charmingly situated and well designed **Freehold Detached Villa Residence,** erected according to the plans and under the supervision of an eminent architect, and which will be sold with **vacant possession.**

The accommodation is as follows: On the Ground Floor—Vestibule and Entrance Hall, Dining Room, 15ft. 3in. by 12ft. 9in.; Drawing Room, 15ft. 3in. by 14ft. 9in.; Kitchen, 16ft. 3in. by 13ft.; Scullery, 12ft. 9in. by 8ft. 9in.; Lavatory, 2 W.C.'s, Larder, and Coals. On the First Floor—Five Bedrooms, 17ft. by 13ft., 17ft. by 13ft., 13ft. by 12ft. 9in., 13ft. by 10ft. 6in., and 11ft. 9in. by 11ft. 9in.; and Bath Room (hot and cold); and on the Upper Floor Nursery, 13ft. 9in. by 13ft. 9in., and Servants' Bedroom. The House is very substantially built, and of a pleasing elevation. It stands on high ground, and commands magnificent views on all sides. It is close to St. Hilda's Church, and is within a few minutes' walk of the Ravenscar Railway Station and the Raven Hall Hotel. Water is laid on from the new mains. The enclosed Garden has a frontage of 100 feet to Raven Hall Road, and a return frontage of 120 feet to Crag Hill Road, to both of which roads the building line is set back 25 feet. The superficial area of the site is 1,355 square yards.

There is an accommodation road on the westerly side.

N.B.—The provisions of the 16th condition as to completion by instalments do not apply to Lot 42, but arrangements can, if desired, be made for payment of four-fifths of the purchase money by instalments extending over a period not exceeding ten years.

Advertising the sale of Crag Hill Villa

CHAPTER TWO

EXPECTATIONS

A new century brought a very different industry to the village. On the site of the old Alum Quarry Messrs. B Whitaker and Sons Ltd of Horsforth built a brickwork yard, with two chimneys dominating the beautiful landscape. The entrepreneurs recognised an immediate outlet for their product and hoped to supply the necessary materials required to build the many properties on this new development. The name Ravenscar appeared on the face of each brick. The outlook for employment was at an all-time high and the residents anticipated a bright future of prosperity.

Whitaker's Brickyard

In January 1901 the whole country plunged into deep mourning on the death of Queen Victoria. To show their respect householders painted picture frames, mirrors and even furniture, black.

During the summer of that year the 34th sale took place and a linen map dated July 1st showed properties already constructed. These included houses in Loring Road and the New Villa on Raven Hall Road. Three shelters on the Marine Esplanade were marked as covered seats, each divided into four seating areas separated by wooden partitions with windows affording visitors magnificent sea views. These also gave protection from prevailing winds, rain and even scorching sun. Although the elaborate drainage and sewerage system had been completed, Crag Villa, the Church Villas and High Peak Farm (Church Farm) were not connected; consequently householders had to dispose of their own waste. Good vegetable crops were guaranteed! There were two main drains with offshoots. One started in Hammond Road behind the New Villa, crossed Station Road, then turned right along Marine Esplanade and then continued to the sewer outfall between Raven Hall Hotel and Sea View Villa. The second began its journey in Church Road beyond Church Villas, included the new houses and the Post Office, veered left down Loring Road with one manhole estimated at twenty-five feet deep. It passed under the railway line and collected sewerage from Station Square, Station House and the Vicarage, and was channelled right along Marine Esplanade to a second outfall no more than fifteen feet below the cliff top.

At Station Square four shop outlets were planned but in fact this only came to fruition at No 4. Numbers 1, 2, and 3 were opened as a high-class boarding house known as 'Ravenscar House' with thirty-six rooms. It was open all year and managed by Mrs Harris.

Senior figures living in the village at this time were Charles Wrightson - foreman road maker; Emma Denham of Crag Villa; Robert Gilmour - agent and surveyor; George Ismay - foreman brickmaker; Harry Blott - coastguard; Auton Leopold Becker - clergyman; William Nesfield - farmer at High Peak Farm, and John Forster - the station master who would soon be replaced by John Easton.

Above: Ravenscar station porter

Below: Sale board at Station Square

The village was also served by a post office situated at Church Road Farm. Richard Jackson, a farmer and joiner, took on the role of sub-postmaster assisted by his wife Diana and daughter Martha (Nellie). This was a busy life as they worked the Post Office seven days a week. The opening hours were 8am to 8pm on weekdays and 8.30am to 10am Sundays. Christmas day for this family was a normal working day,

Richard tended his animals and Martha delivered the eagerly awaited mail, while Diana prepared a late Christmas dinner of roast goose with trimmings and plum pudding. A rare sight was the wooden postbox attached to the property and accessed by several stone steps.

Footpath and steps set into Undercliff Gardens

Photograph taken from the steps towards Cliff House

Sadly Mr Rusby did not survive to greet the new century and only enjoyed his new villa for two years. His widow Mary and daughter Beatrice continued to reside at Sea View Villa, later to be known as Cliff House.

A weekly routine for many locals would be a walk down to the rocks via a footpath below Raven Hall Hotel, or probably the quickest route would be to explore the new steps and Undercliff Gardens which descended from the cliff top near Station Square. During the summer months from 15th June to 15th September a fee of 2d to cover maintenance was charged.

The youngsters enjoyed collecting winkles, and these live shellfish would then be cast into a pot of boiling water. The slug-like creatures were drawn from their shells using a pin from the sewing box, and relished with vinegar, bread and butter.

The adults would have their eyes on richer pickings from shipwrecks and items washed overboard in rough seas. They didn't have long to wait; during the spring of 1903 the trawler 'Puritan' struck rocks at Peak in bad visibility and came ashore. The crew of twelve took to their small boat and after drifting for several hours the Scarborough trawler 'Hero' took them on board. The stricken vessel however lost its large haul of fish and became a total wreck.

Monthly auctions continued the same year with extra sales publicity to whet the appetite of clients. Amongst the attractions was a tranquil walk along Tan Beck, with newly laid footpaths and bridges over the meandering stream and miniature waterfalls. 'British rainfall' provided a real boost with statistics; Ravenscar had thirty-five fewer rainy days consecutively in 1900 and 1901 than Scarborough or Whitby. The relatively new Golf Links laid out on the edge of the moors would be an added amenity, and the following fees were advertised: Day tickets, 1/-; Weekly, 2/6; Four weeks, 5/- and Yearly 21/-. The cliff-top hotel site a few hundred yards north of Raven Hall Hotel was not sold, despite being advertised extensively. On the original plans all plots of land offered for sale were coloured light pink and those disposed of were coloured green. The roads already made and those which the vendors agreed to construct, were coloured yellow.

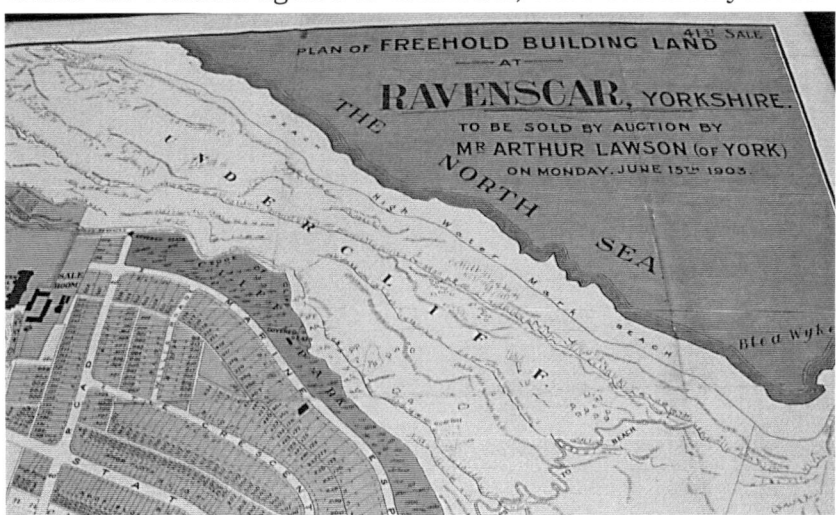

Section of the plan for the 41st sale

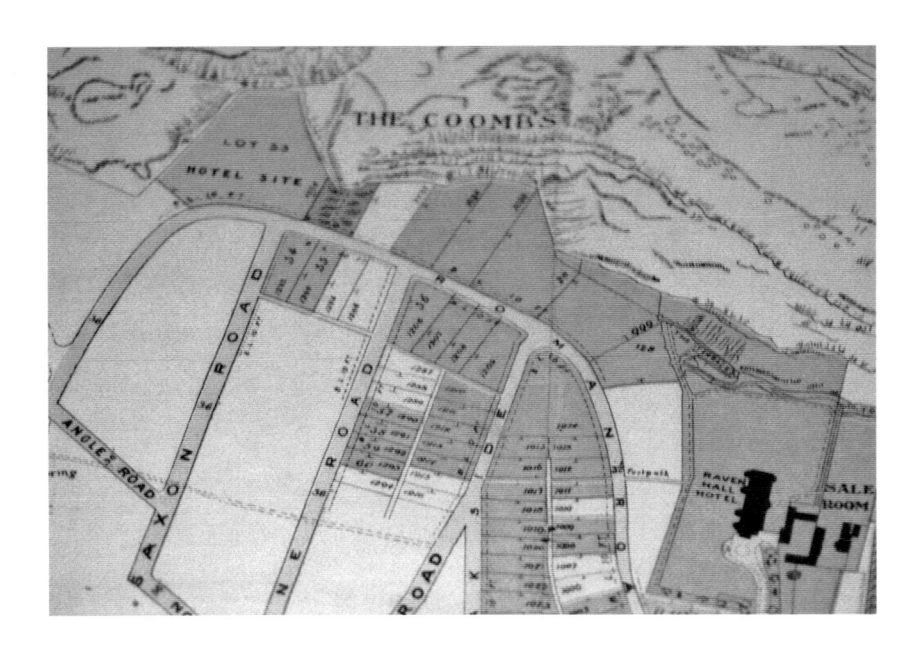

Above: Unsold hotel site

Wreck of the 'Kaiser'

Ravenscar Mill at the time of writing

The following year a repeat disaster happened when a cargo ship the 'Kaiser' ran aground in dense fog, and like the 'Puritan' all aboard were rescued.

One summer's day in 1904, Mr and Mrs Bush from Mill Farm decided to go for a drive. After the doors were locked they set off in earnest, oblivious to the fact that a stranger was watching their every move. Upon returning, the wonderful day was shattered. A door had been forcibly opened, rooms ransacked, and precious possessions stolen which included a gold bracelet with a half-sovereign attached and a gold dress ring set with opals and diamonds. Also a gold watch chain was taken. The scoundrel was later apprehended at Whitby with the stolen goods on his person. He admitted stealing from Mr and Mrs Bush and when charged he replied, "I was out of work and hungry or I should not have done it." He was later sent for trial in Northallerton.

Every New Year the villagers looked forward to an annual party at Raven Hall, which was organised by the manageress Mrs Constance.

The local paper of 1908 described the event thus: *'Tea was provided about 5pm and the remainder of the evening was spent in listening to songs, etc., given by Mr Jarvis Sanders, Miss Constance, Miss Whitaker and others, whilst a large Christmas tree was relieved of its many useful presents, which were given to the children. To conclude the evening dancing was taken up with spirit to the accompaniment of Master Coulson, from Staintondale. Coals and other gifts were distributed by Mrs Constance to the widows and aged people.'*

During February yet another vessel the 'Mandalay' succumbed to the dense fog that prevailed in the bay. Fortunately all crew came ashore safely.

Wreck of the Mandalay

Fox hunting was a very popular and necessary blood sport. Farmers relied on the hunt and gamekeepers to keep the fox population down. They hoped for a successful season in order to protect their poultry and young lambs. Desperate for food the cunning creature would even carry away the domestic cat! The Staintondale Hunt held an annual dinner using local hostelries, which included the Raven Hall, the Shepherds Arms, Hayburn Wyke and Scalby Mills Hotel. Diners included hound walkers, gamekeepers, and members of the committee.

The ultimate aim was to attract a good field with excellent runs and a high number of kills. One day, young Bill, a local farmer's son decided to join the meet, and was thrilled to witness his first kill. The Master walked over to him and with two fingers daubed the youngster's cheeks with the unlucky victim's blood. The Master proceeded to skin the brush of the dog fox which he handed to Bill, who promptly put it in his jacket pocket. Back home he proudly presented the tail to his mother for pickling. Eventually, having been stuffed, it took pride of place in the hallway. Foxes sometimes outwitted their pursuers and went to ground. On one occasion a crafty old boy took refuge in a disused jet mine.

Entrance to a disused jet mine at Ravenscar

By the end of 1909 there was evidence that Ravenscar Estate Company was in financial difficulties. A schedule in the Deeds of 'Corbie' referred to *An Instrument of Appointment of Receiver dated October 8th 1909. Debenture holders appointed Thomas Wilkinson as receiver.*

The majority of properties that had been built were occupied by tenants, not the business people who owned them. Farms held by the Estate Company were sold off to prospective buyers who in turn leased them to farmers.

Sydney H. Carter

During 1910 a very prominent figure arrived in Ravenscar and took up residence at Crag Villa. Sydney Hammond Carter moved to the village with his wife Amy from Menston in Bradford West Yorkshire. He was the son of Bennett Carter a theatrical promoter who employed a large workforce to run entertainment venues in Bradford. Prior to moving to the east coast, Sydney adopted the pioneering cinematograph, showing silent films. He went further, setting up a company leasing cinemas in the area and this was later to become the New Century Film Company.

The registered office was at 18 Drake Street Bradford, advertising 'Hirofilms'. This was a time in cinema history when almost every street corner had some form of picture house. Sydney Carter was at the forefront with this new form of entertainment and showed films at the Coliseum in Leeds. A newspaper review from the Leeds and Yorkshire Mercury dated April 9th 1907 states:

'The New Century pictures at the Coliseum continue to run their animated way, and the public, who know a good thing when they see it, patronise the show in no half-hearted fashion..........the beholder may shift his vision within the moment to the river swamps of central Africa, where hippopotamus makes its lair. There is humour visualised, too; and the show as a whole is one of the best seen in the city.'

The following week New Century Pictures opened yet another cinema. The Yorkshire post of April 16th 1907 gave a glowing review:

'The Grand Assembly Rooms in New Briggate, Leeds, which have undergone complete renovation with fresh structural arrangements, now present the appearance of a modern place of amusement, equalling in some respects more pretentious establishments of the kind. The rooms were reopened last night with the production of Mr. Sydney Carter's New Century Animated Pictures, which had recently such a long run of success at the Coliseum. The entertainment comprised a succession of pictures in a series of highly amusing sketches,.......... supplemented by more serious subjects, and with the constant changes of programme which are promised by the manager, a dull moment from beginning to end can hardly be imagined.'

In March 1910, the Cricket Club at the neighbouring village of Staintondale, held a social evening attended by almost 100 people and the event was reported in the local paper.

'The ladies of the Dale provided and presided over an excellent supper at which 97 sat down. Messrs. Hunter and Coulson presided at the piano lent by Mrs Coulson. Dancing, songs, games, etc., were indulged in and the party did not break up until daylight'. This goes to show that villagers certainly were not bored with their lot in life at that time!

Village children with Church Farm, church and Church Villas in the background

A year after the death of Edward VII, the Coronation of King George V and Queen Mary took place on June 22nd 1911. A jubilant nation had every confidence that this Monarch would be a leading light to all. This was echoed in Ravenscar with a full day of celebrations, commencing with a commemorative service at St Hilda's Church. As so many wanted to attend it was necessary to provide extra seating. Afterwards, Mr Archibald Marshall, the grandson of William Hammond planted a Coronation oak tree in the churchyard. The honour of hoisting the Union Jack was given to Mr Charles Wrightson, who lived at Church Villas. Afterwards, everyone made their way across the road to Church Farm, where Mr Atkinson had made a field available for the various sports and games. The most popular of these games proved to be 'The Kicking Donkey'. The newly arrived businessman, Sydney H. Carter, directed the children in an open air performance of 'Robin Hood' to great acclaim. Mrs Carter made some impressive costumes which added a further touch of professionalism to the play. The villagers now headed to the schoolroom, where each child was presented with a Coronation mug before refreshments were served. This delightful day was rounded off with a bonfire followed by music and dancing, provided by Mr Easton, the stationmaster.

Sea View Villa was sold to a Mrs Eliza Wray, a cinematography supplier and wife of Cecil Wray from the Wray Film Agency. No doubt this would seem strange to villagers having two film makers in their midst.

RAVENSCAR.

On the MARINE ESPLANADE.

LOT 5   A charmingly situated and well designed **Freehold Detached Villa Residence,** known as "Corby," erected according to the plans and under the supervision of an eminent architect, and which will be sold with **vacant possession.**

The accommodation is as follows: On the Ground Floor—Vestibule and Entrance Hall, 18ft. by 12ft. 9in.; Dining Room, 14ft. 3in. by 13ft.; Drawing Room, 15ft. 3in. by 12ft. 6in.; Morning Room, 13ft. by 9ft. 6in.; Kitchen, 13ft. by 12ft. 9in.; Good Scullery, Lavatory, 2 W.C.'s; Drying Room and Coals. On the First Floor—Six Bedrooms, 13ft. 6in. by 13ft. 6in.; 16ft. 6in. by 10ft. 9in.; 12ft. by 13ft.; 15ft. 3in. by 10ft. 4in.; 13ft. 3in. by 13ft. 3in., and 13ft. 6in. by 12ft. 6in.; and on the Upper Floor—Two Bedrooms, each 17ft. by 9ft.; Bath Room, Large Store Room and Box Cupboard. The House is very substantially built and commands magnificent sea views, and is close to the Railway Station. Water is laid on from the new mains. The enclosed Garden has a frontage of 68 feet to the Marine Esplanade, to which the building line is set back 15 feet, the depth on the North-Westerly side being 99 feet, and on the South-Easterly side 96 feet. And the adjoining unfenced Plot No.10 on the Estate plan with a frontage of 40 feet widening to 52 feet at the back, and a depth of 125 feet, and on which an additional house could if desired be erected, will be included in the Sale, thus making the total frontage to the Marine Esplanade, 108 feet. The superficial area of the whole site is 1376 square yards.

There is an accommodation road at the back.

N.B.—No extra charge will be made to the purchaser of this lot for the cost of paving, &c., of the Marine Esplanade opposite the lot, nor for constructing the sewer to which the house is connected.

Sale notice advertising 'Corbie'

The Wesleyan Chapel at Peak Side was little used apart from the popular Harvest Festival service. Mr Wrightson, the estate manager was very involved with running nearby Staintondale Wesleyan Chapel Sunday School. At the annual New Year's Day party he was thanked for all his hard work.

On New Year's Day in 1913 a thief decided he would have a prosperous New Year by breaking into all the railway stations between Ravenscar and Scalby near Scarborough. Only a small amount of cash and postage stamps were taken.

Mr Carter of Crag Hill purchased 'Corbie' plus three adjacent plots from the Ravenscar Estate Limited and Mr Thomas Wilkinson the receiver. In the conveyance dated February 12th it stipulated:

'Not to erect or allow to be erected upon any pieces of the land hereby conveyed at any time hereafter any shop workshop or manufactory nor any beer shop, public house or hotel for the sale of malt or spiritous liquors or any other building than a private dwelling house.'

Although all these restrictions were specified in the conveyance, Mr Carter was granted permission to erect a suitable studio for the purpose of taking and developing cinematograph films. However, he did not neglect his main cinema business interests in Bradford and Leeds.

***

CHAPTER THREE

COMINGS AND GOINGS

A few miles inland in the quaint village of Hackness a young couple, Jonty and Vi (my grandparents), were planning a future together. The only obstacle in their way was the shortage of farms to rent in the area. Jonty was running his late father's farm at Hilla Green and during the previous year had acquired a pony and trap, two cart horses, two cows, poultry, a wagon, one plough and a set of harrows. A few small items he needed along with many others, were a muck fork, hayfork, shovel, yard brush, milk buckets and a three-legged milking stool; why only three you may ask, because the fourth is the udder!

Meanwhile Vi, daughter of the village postmistress with no farming experience whatsoever, gathered together furniture and the usual bottom-drawer linens. Fully aware that she was not prepared for life as a farmer's wife, Vi enrolled on a butter and cheese making course at the creamery in Garforth, West Riding of Yorkshire. Several times throughout the busy farming calendar, she would help out on local farms at hay time and harvest to grasp more understanding of farm life.

After eighteen months the waiting was over and a Mr Lotherington who owned farms in the Ravenscar area offered them Church Farm. However, the land was in such poor condition, that, as a concession, they were granted the first year rent free.

Eventually the joyful occasion arrived on April 13th 1913. The bells were ringing at St Peter's Church Hackness, Johnson Robinson entered followed by his beautiful bride Violet Hubbard for their marriage ceremony. Afterwards an elated couple and guests enjoyed afternoon tea in the schoolroom, but shortly said farewell to family and friends. The newlyweds headed off for a new life in Ravenscar leaving behind a village full of childhood memories. They travelled by pony and trap from the low-lying village of Hackness, up the steep incline to Suffield through mixed woodland, which was the protective haunt of pheasants, deer and numerous native red squirrels. A few miles ahead there was a noticeable change in the surrounding countryside; stone walls replaced hawthorn hedgerows and trees were few and far between leading to open moorland. Almost there, they passed the road to Bell Hill Farm and Danesdale where brothers William and Albert Cross farmed. Approaching the disused mill which had already lost its sails, Springfield Farm could be seen across the field on the right where Mr and Mrs Heslington lived. Taking a backward glance, the new arrivals would be rewarded with a splendid view down the coastline to Flamborough Head.

Johnson and Violet Robinson's Wedding

The pond on their left was once a stone quarry until one morning workers arrived to find all their tools under several feet of water; the unfortunate fellows had disturbed an underground spring. Mr and Mrs Bush with their children Arthur and Jessie, had already left Mill Farm to run a bakery in Hull. The new occupants were Mr and Mrs Miles and their daughters Ruby and Pearl. Ruby worked across the road at the poultry farm named Moorfield House, managed by Mr Pyne.

This property had previously been known as 'Raven Hill Inn' nicknamed 'Blue Robin' by pub regulars, because the barmaid always donned a blue pinafore. Within minutes Jonty and Vi arrived at their new abode, Church Farm.

The happy couple arrive at Ravenscar

Jonty faced an enormous task with seventy acres of neglected land to rejuvenate. The first priority was sowing turnips and oats to feed the livestock. Help was at hand, and following an old tradition, neighbouring farmers gave a day's ploughing to newcomers. Potatoes also had to be planted without delay to avoid the risk of 'June jumpers' (a weak crop as a result of late planting). Vi, now a thrifty farmer's wife settled into a weekly routine starting with washing day on Monday. Clothes were soaked for several hours, wrung out and placed in a tub of hot water. Each article was rubbed with a large bar of soap, then 'poshed' and rinsed twice. Whites were boiled in a large copper, heated from beneath by a coal fire. A dolly blue bag was added to the second rinse, not for too long, otherwise the washing would be tinged blue.

Wet clothes and sheets were fed into a hand-turned, wrought iron mangle with huge wooden rollers, which squeezed out water leaving pressed garments ready to hang on the washing line. Ravenscar breezes made sure everything dried quickly.

Tuesday morning after breakfast Vi mixed a large bowl of pastry and using lard saved from pig killing day, made a weekly batch of jam tarts, treacle tarts and apple pies. Jam sponge or currant cakes were an extra treat for hard-working labourers. After tea the farmer's wife didn't have much relaxation, clothes were repaired, socks darned, and buttons sewn on.

Wednesday, along with the daily tasks of feeding poultry, collecting eggs and cooking meals, ironing also beckoned. An old folded blanket covered with a clean sheet was placed on the kitchen table; flat irons heated in front of a coal fire in the kitchen range were spat on and the sizzling steam indicated the iron was ready for use.

Heating flat irons on the kitchen range

Thursday, without extra chores, was spent sowing vegetables in the garden including cabbage, cauliflower, lettuce and onions. Peas and beans were planted later. Every two weeks or so, a shopping trip to Scarborough would be a welcome change for her, but she was ever mindful of returning in good time to make dinner.

By Friday a 'hen out of lay' was needed for the next meal. This was done by making sure two fingers could not be inserted between the back end bones. Jonty had the unpleasant task of wringing its neck. He quickly handed the 'ficking' bird to Vi for plucking, it was then passed over a shovel of lit methylated spirits to remove any surplus feathers or hair before being dressed. As the chicken was cooking Vi prepared dough to make bread for the coming week.

Saturday was house cleaning day: wearing a coarse apron made from hessian over her pinafore, she tackled the filthiest jobs of the week such as black leading the hearth, beating rugs with a besom, scrubbing doorsteps and finishing them off with a covering of donkey stone. These chalk like stones manufactured in Lancashire were produced in a range of colours which enhanced doorsteps, creating a warm welcome to the home. However, on rainy days this extra effort was short lived.

The Sabbath day was widely observed by attending church with only essential jobs being undertaken, namely feeding livestock and milking cows. Everybody looked forward to dinner; the smell from the oven being a treat in itself. Yorkshire pudding with beef and onion gravy traditionally served as a first course, was followed by roast beef, roast or mashed potatoes and vegetables. During the afternoon it was customary to take a leisurely walk. No doubt our couple would head for the cliff top to view the stranded steamer 'Coronation' which had run aground a few weeks earlier. Back in February a large quantity of coal was thrown overboard and the lucky locals gathered up a bounty of cheap winter fuel. After an unsuccessful attempt to tow the vessel off the rocks, all was abandoned until later. Before the wedding, Vi had received a postcard dated 10th March from a friend staying at Ravenscar House; written on the reverse *'Hope you like this P.C. Since it was taken, it has come much nearer the cliff'*. They could now see the wreck for themselves. The ship was eventually towed away in September.

Above: The 'Coronation' viewed from the cliff

Below: The 'Coronation' stranded at Ravenscar

Now settled in his new surroundings, Jonty and other members of the farming community continued with an unchanging cycle in the countryside calendar. As lambs frolicked in the fields suddenly the swallows appeared, and within days the first cuckoo was heard, familiar to everyone by its distinctive call. In the last week of April these observations were recorded in a farmer's diary. During the first fortnight of May, cattle and horses were turned out and wallowed in their freedom, galloping uncontrollably for several minutes before settling down to graze, savouring every blade of fresh grass.

Farmhouse kitchen range and milking stool.

By the end of June sheep shearing time had begun. Firstly the flock, apart from young lambs, were 'docked'; all locks of dung-coated wool (dags) had to be removed. The farmer held the sheep in a sitting position using one arm and with shears poised in the other hand he expertly clipped, until eventually the fleece fell away in one piece. Individually they were rolled and tied. Hundreds of these bundles were transported by train to the West Riding woollen mills.

As hay time arrived, the sweet scent of new mown grass drying in the meadows filled the air. Fortunate farmers owned a horse-drawn reaper, while smallholders mowed by hand using scythes. After regular turning with a wooden rake, aided by sunshine, the hay became completely dry ready to be gathered into haycocks and finally led to the main stack to be used for winter feed. Turnip hoeing was fitted in around this time and, weather permitting, all would be completed by the beginning of August. Within three to four weeks the golden cornfields were ripe for harvesting. Before the binder could enter, the field needed 'opening out' and a strip of corn was cut with a scythe around the whole perimeter and loose corn gathered into hand-tied sheaves. All moving machine parts were oiled and twine was threaded through the needle, the horses were then yoked up to the binder, ready to go. The harvested corn travelled up a canvas conveyor to the metal packers. When enough heads for a sheaf were collected a clever mechanism came into action knotting and cutting the twine before casting the bundle clear of the binder. Sheaves were gathered into stooks, which were stood north to south in order to assist the drying process. After church bells had rung on three consecutive Sundays, corn was ready for leading. Using pitchforks the sheaves were tossed from the wagon to an experienced stacker working on his knees. Cut ends were placed to the outside with heads pointing inwards; built in this manner, the stack was surprisingly waterproof. When harvest finished it was time to plough and harrow, preparing soil for drilling the following year's wheat crop.

Mr Stubbs of Low Peak experienced a farmer's worst nightmare when a haystack valued at £60 overheated. On the top of the stack a large plume of smoke was noticed and a telegram was sent to the Scarborough fire station reading *'A large hayrick on fire near Ravenscar Hotel'*. Willing locals carried buckets of water and within an hour the fire engine arrived. After three hours the fire was extinguished with two thirds of the stack saved.

At this time in history, steam was an energy source used on the railways and in road making, as well as for driving threshing machines on the farm. These were hired with the contractor for one day. On these occasions, up to ten farm hands were supplied from nearby farms. When the sheaves were fed into the thresher it separated corn from straw and discarded the husks (chaff). The worker feeding sheaves into an open-topped thresher had to be extremely careful not to lose his balance, as did happen on rare occasions and fatalities occurred. Hessian sacks were attached on the side to catch sixteen stone of grain, with a winding up barrow raised to shoulder height assisting the worker who carried the load. For selling purposes oats were weighed off at twelve stone, barley at sixteen, and wheat at eighteen stone. A large sheet was laid underneath the machine to catch chaff: this along with straw was stored in a barn for fodder and bedding. The busy farmer's wife and helpers provided a well-earned dinner for the workers.

Field of stooks

Now into autumn, it was time for lambs to be sold at Seamer market, but not before the best gimmers had been selected for future breeding. One farmer's philosophy was to stick with ewes 'cos after 10 o'clock the Lord Is My Shepherd'. At this time of year there was an excellent trade with good prices. Lambs fetched from twenty-nine to forty-seven shillings each. When the sale ended, drovers herded animals from the auction mart along Seamer Road to Falsgrave, down Victoria Road and into Dean Road to their journey's end at William Street abattoir.

Wash tub and posher

Supplies of bacon and ham were running low at the farm kitchen, so a date was arranged with two local men who specialised in pig killing. On the run up to this day, in addition to their ordinary diet, pigs would be fed boiled potatoes not fit for human consumption. Gradually, ground barley was introduced into the feed, this being the best food to 'fatten them up'. The squealing pig was led into a straw-covered yard; a metal punch placed on the vital spot and down came the mallet killing the animal instantly. Quickly the throat was cut, blood gushed into a bucket and was later used to make black puddings. The dead pig was hauled into a tub of boiling water and scrapers were used to remove all hairs. With a hook, claws were then pulled away from the trotters. Its carcass was strung up in an outbuilding and all inedible pieces discarded.

Winding barrow

Indoors, housewives were ready with sharpened knives to cut up the two pieces of leaf fat (a dense fat that collects round the kidneys) with other pork trimmings, which were rendered down into scraps. The fat was poured into an enamel bucket and when set became high-grade lard. With a smell of blood in the air, wary horses refused to pass the killing ground, having to be led from the stable to a water-trough. The salting of pork was a necessary process and after three or four weeks the sides and hams were hung from ceiling hooks. Pork based meals were normal for at least two weeks. These included liver and onions, pork pies and scraps. The head and trotters were boiled until the meat fell from the bones and after removing gristle, the jellied gravy and meat were poured into a mould to make brawn; this was served cold for breakfast or tea.

As November approached, a ram had his lower chest painted with rud before he was ready to make his grand entrance into a field of ewes. Sniffing the air he approached the flock looking for his first willing girl. During the following two or three weeks it would be a busy time for this lad who covered perhaps forty ewes.

Away from the farming calendar, Miss Newstead, Headmistress of Ravenscar School for nearly ten years, decided to leave and move on to a new post. She lodged with Mr and Mrs Wrightson, at Church Villas and later, Ravenscar House in Station Square. Scholars and friends gave the popular teacher a gold pendant set with pearls and amethysts; Reverend D. Scott, who made the presentation at the Institute, thanked Miss Newstead for her hard work and enthusiasm. Miss Dalkin from Northallerton was appointed her successor and she too lodged at Ravenscar House until her parents Robert and Mary Dalkin, along with two other daughters, Miss Mary Ann and Miss Roberta, came to live at 'Dunelm' in Raven Hall Road. Whilst Mary Ann was housekeeper, her sister Roberta worked for Oxendale Catalogue Company in Manchester. Another leading figure also left the village: stationmaster Mr Easton transferred to Slingsby. He, his wife and nine children left a massive gap in the community, having lived there for eleven years. To show their appreciation, everyone clubbed together purchasing a silver tea service, six spoons and a pair of sugar tongs. Staff from Whitaker's brickworks wished to make their own contributions, in the form of an ebony walking stick and pipe. The Vicar presented these gifts at the church reading room. Mr C. Bradley took over as stationmaster. Mr Thompson, the brickyard manager left Raven Hall Road and moved to 4 Station Square and took over the grocer's shop.

Above: Raven Hall Road

Below: Postman at Church Villas

Following the death of Richard Jackson on November 5th 1913 aged 65; his widow Diana took over as sub-postmistress. She received new instructions from the Post

51

Office regarding the packaging of parcels. These new regulations applied to eggs, liquids, china, butter and sharp instruments. Fish and meat had to be packed with care to prevent any leakage soiling other items. Special rules applied to game.

'Game is accepted without covering, and with a neck label only attached for the address, provided that no blood or other liquid is exuding or likely to exude, and that the game itself is not so 'high' as to taint other parcels..........'.

As Christmas celebrations approached, nobody in the village had any idea of what would hit the country, and indeed the whole world, during the following year.

A moment captured in time. Mr Jackson collecting kindling in Ravenscar along with his daughter Nellie – under protest! c.1900

***

CHAPTER FOUR

UNSETTLING TIMES

Unaware of the gloomy times that lay ahead, locals were enthusiastically holding events to raise money for an extension to the church. On May Day 1914 an appreciative audience enjoyed a concert given at the Church Institute. The opening selection was a pianoforte solo by Miss Pearl Miles. This event was covered in the local press:

'The Glees, 'The Torpedo and the Whale' (soloist, Mr Carter) and 'The Bells of St Michael's Tower' were well sung by Mrs Hopkins, Misses Beeforth, M. A. Dalkin, and Hunter (sopranos) Misses Carter and Dalkin (contraltos).

Rev. D. A. Scott (tenor), and Messrs Carter and Hunter (bass), with their humorous rendering of the concerted item 'The Wild Man of Borneo' achieved marked success..........

Mr Carter delighted his audience with a series of one minute humorous sketches.

A group of children conducted by Miss Dalkin, sang nicely 'Cherry Ripe', 'It was a Lover and his Lass', 'Golden Slumbers' and 'Land of my Fathers'.

The song, 'The Miller and the Maid' was tastefully sung by Miss Beeforth.

Miss L. Shaw as a Bavarian wanderer sang in a sweet and unaffected style 'Buy a Broom' and received a vociferous encore.

Miss Ruby Miles and Mrs Bradley accompanied.'

Parishioners of Ravenscar and Staintondale were excited about the formation of their new parish when St Hilda's Church and Churchyard were consecrated on July 29th by the Bishop of Hull.

St Hilda's Church

Rev. D. A. Scott, who had been curate in charge, was expected to become the new vicar. Mrs Becker had worked hard raising money for an endowment fund, to provide for a future vicar's salary. She was the widow of Rev. Anton Leopold Becker, who ministered without a salary for eight years prior to his death in 1907 at the age of seventy.

Rev. James Willoughby B.A., predecessor to Rev. D. A. Scott, with the church choir

The Church, Institute and Churchyard, were a gift from Ravenscar Estate Company to the Parish. This included the furniture and fittings. The altar was donated by Mrs Becker. Mr Carter arranged for his father's pipe organ to be removed from the family residence in Bradford and be installed in Ravenscar Church.

As well as commitments in his business life, Sydney Carter and his wife Amy fostered three siblings, Jack, Frank and Molly Green, from Menston in the West Riding of Yorkshire. However Molly soon returned to her mother. Both Jack, and his brother Frank, remained in Ravenscar and were brought up as part of the family at Crag Hill.

Events quickly came to an abrupt end when war was declared between Britain and Germany on the 4th of August, following the invasion of Belgium. Within four months, over two hundred thousand Belgian refugees had arrived on our shores and were re-homed throughout the country - including the east coast and Ravenscar. The villagers had to say goodbye to many brave young men, who went to fight for King and Country. It was understood that Frank Wrightson was among the first local men to volunteer. Meanwhile farmers stayed behind to work the land; consequently, Jonty remained at home and was appointed Special Constable. Part of his duties included patrolling the village at night, checking that all properties were in total darkness: not even a flickering candle was permitted. As life in the village continued, some fundraising events were in aid of the Belgian refugees.

The Great War moved frighteningly close as daylight broke on December 16th about 8am. Lasting for thirty minutes, an enemy battle cruiser and an armoured cruiser bombarded Scarborough from the sea killing eighteen men, women and children. Four people lost their lives at No 2 Wykeham Street. At the same time two battle cruisers shelled Whitby - again casualties were reported. Ravenscar, lying between the two chosen targets, escaped unscathed; but residents must have heard the menacing sound of gunfire and waited in trepidation wondering what was about to happen. Reports of these dreadful attacks, would reach the stationmaster when the first trains from Whitby and Scarborough arrived.

Tragedy at Number 2 Wykeham Street, Scarborough

Mr Dalkin had recently moved to 'Dunelm' but sadly only enjoyed the breathtaking views of Robin Hood's Bay and the moors for one year, before he died on February 11th 1915. His death was the first entry in the Church of England's new burial register, but daughters Miss Dalkin, the head teacher, and Miss Mary Ann, continued to be two of the central figures in social life.

Spring arrived and Mr W.B. Cross made the news when a cow adopted two motherless lambs, who ran up a strategically placed wooden plank to suckle. It was a rare sight indeed and would be a great help during the busy lambing time.

By November, three local farms, Grange Farm, Rudda Farm and Bent Rigg Farm including a copse, were auctioned off at the George Hotel in Scarborough. However, all three were withdrawn, until at a later date, Mr Micklethwaite bought Rudda Farm and Mr Lotherington acquired Bent Rigg Farm - including the wooded area. At this secluded spot he chose to build a holiday cottage with an exceptional view down the coast to Scarborough.

Local men who had joined up were not forgotten, as Peakside Refreshment Rooms decided to hold a social event to raise money for Christmas parcels. An evening packed with a varied programme of entertainment commenced with the National Anthem followed by singing, recitations, games and dancing. Those who participated were Miss Beeforth, Mrs Currie, Miss M.A. Dalkin, Miss Duck, Mrs Hall, Miss Harland, Mrs Harrison, Mrs Thompson and Miss Wright. Soldiers stationed in the village also took part and refreshments were provided by Mrs Lloyd.

Throughout these unsettling times, much of the social life revolved around church functions and periodically Miss Dalkin would arrange concerts at the school. At a vestry meeting, the new incumbent, Rev. E. J. Clark B.A., nominated Mr S. H. Carter as his warden and Mr Charles Wrightson was elected the people's warden. Miss Dalkin, an obvious choice for vestry clerk, was duly appointed.

Messrs. Easton, Hilton, R.T. Hunter, Miles, Pyne, Robinson, Thompson and Wedgwood, were chosen to form the Parochial Church Council. The vicar thanked the wardens, sidesmen, choirs, sewing parties, and all who helped at socials and concerts, for their support. Rev. Clark followed Rev. Scott into a semi-detached house in Church Road, named for a short time 'Waterloo Villa', but better known as 'Moorcroft'. However, this was not deemed suitable. With the approval of the Ecclesiastical Commissioners, a plot of land was purchased in Robin Hood Road for thirty pounds. It was their intention to start building the new vicarage in the spring of 1918. The vicar planned regular 'Magic Lantern' shows in the Church Institute, to boost funds for the chancel. He controlled the lantern whilst his wife accompanied the singing. However, the piano would not hold its tuning, so once again Mr Carter resolved the problem by giving a brand new instrument.

Members of the church wasted no time in arranging another concert. Miss Pearl Miles again opened the proceedings by giving a virtuoso performance of Chopin's Polonaise in A flat. The chorus party sang 'Four and Twenty Blackbirds' and Mr Carter encouraged the audience to whistle and twitter like birds. Fourteen-year-old Grace Thompson who lived at the family-run grocer's shop in Station Square, played a piano solo for the first time in public.

Off duty soldiers, Sergeant Jones and Privates Thompson, Levitt and Wyatt were also eager to be involved in the show.

Children looking forward to their summer holidays gave a school concert to which their parents were invited. They staged an impressive show of songs and recitations, under the watchful eye of Miss Dalkin. Wilfred Hodgson, Jack Beeforth, Clive Wrightson, William (Billy) Lloyd and Lot Coultas took part in a sketch 'Alfred and the Cakes'. Other performers were Lucy Thompson, Harry Gale, Lena Currie, George Wedgwood, Billy Stubbs, Lawrence Duck, Norah Hodgson, Eva Ward, Isabel Beeforth, Jessie French, Annie Ward, Harriett Lightfoot, Noel Wrightson, and Tom Lightfoot.

However, it was not all play time, as during the holidays, children would be expected to do menial tasks for their parents.

Ravenscar school children c.1916

Standing at the back: - Miss Dalkin and Jane Duck
Back row: - Gertrude Ward, Beatrice Ward, Annie Ward, Hannah Lightfoot, (not known), Lena Currie, Eva Lightfoot, Jessie French. (Half row):- Mary Lightfoot, Edna French, and Isabel Beeforth. Middle row:- Tom Lightfoot, Eva Ward, Norah Hodgson, Lucy Thompson, Jack Green, Hilda Hodgson, Harriet Lightfoot, Grace Thompson, Billy Stubbs, (not known) and George Wedgwood.
Front row: Wilfred Hodgson, Clive Wrightson, William Lloyd, Ernest Thompson, Frank Green, Lawrence Duck and Jack Beeforth.

A week before the new school term, youngsters accompanied by adults gathered heather from the purple clad moorland for the annual heather and flower service. As with the harvest festival two months later, donations were sent to national and military hospitals and any produce considered perishable was given to Scarborough Hospital.

This year, two fundraising events were held for soldiers' Christmas parcels. A whist drive was organised on November 10th, to coincide with the second anniversary of volunteers leaving their everyday surroundings and families, to go to war.

The second event a week later, was a concert arranged by the villagers who joined forces to provide yet another entertaining evening. Halfway through the festivities, Mr Carter presented Mr & Mrs Wrightson with a chiming mantle clock in recognition for their work in the community. The inscription read 'Presented to Mr and Mrs Wrightson as a token of respect from friends at Ravenscar. Christmas 1916'

Mr Wrightson's clock

Cutlery that has survived over a hundred years from Ravenscar House

Heavy snow storms in the first fortnight of April disrupted normal life. Children had an extended weekend when the school closed on Monday and Tuesday, and a sacred concert planned for Palm Sunday, had to be postponed until later. It was also a difficult time for farmers, who had to utilise every spare corner in the buildings to house ewes heavy with lamb and others with offspring less than a week old.

Miss Ruby Miles left the district and moved inland to Bickley. This young woman was such an asset to the community that she received not one presentation, but three in a week. The first gift was a weekend case, presented by Mr Cross on behalf of the Chorus Society: Ruby had been accompanist to the society since its inception. Ernest Thompson, the most senior pupil of the school, handed Miss Miles an ivory manicure set, and in his speech said 'Her fingers had skilfully helped them', so they had chosen an appropriate present. A third item, a silver backed hair brush and tortoiseshell comb, was given to Ruby by Mr Carter, in his capacity as vicar's warden. This young lady had been church organist for over seven years and with her immense versatility would be hard to replace.

Early in June 1917 the locals were enjoying their Sunday afternoon stroll when they had a stark reminder that the country was at war. Just off the coast they noticed a convoy of approximately 40 ships passing by.

During August, the annual 'Sale of Work' organised by church members took place in the Institute. Stallholders sold flowers, cakes, hand-knitted garments, and delicately embroidered linens. Across the road, Mr and Mrs Carter showed their hospitality by providing refreshments at Crag Hill.

Once again it was time for the soldiers' Christmas parcels. This year Miss Dalkin decided to introduce a different type of entertainment and she trained a troupe of 'Black Minstrels'. So popular was the style of programme, that it was repeated by demand ten days later. Members of the troupe were the local schoolchildren who sang 'Oh dem Golden Slippers' 'Go down Moses' 'Down by the Riverside' 'Who's dat a Callin' - amongst other well-known spirituals. An instrumental solo was played by Miss Pattie Cross - including Boccherini's 'Minuet' and Schubert's 'Marche Militaire'.

Apparently, the Staintondale Hunt had not been very successful in their number of kills at this time. So in the interests of food preservation (lambs and poultry) it was necessary to organise a fox drive through Beastcliff, where numbers were increasing rapidly. In the Scarborough Mercury of 28th December 1917 it states:

'No fox was secured, but several were driven to ground after receiving a dose of small shot, to which they would, no doubt, eventually succumb. Good sport was witnessed, and it is hoped that a larger attendance will be secured for the next drive, thereby increasing the chances of a good haul of foxes.'

Another fox cull was organised early in the following year and was reported 15th March 1918:

'Foxes proved numerous ......several got to ground after successfully avoiding the hail of shot which greeted them at every appearance, but three were bowled over and secured, one a vixen heavy with young.'

Badger-baiting was also popular at this time. Let us now leave these horror stories behind. News was emerging about young men who had been absent from the parish for more than two years. William Duck came home on three days' leave during March 1918 after serving on a torpedo destroyer. It was also confirmed that George Beeforth was safe and well. William Lyon of Grange Farm and Thomas Leonard, were both in hospital; but when William was discharged, he was allowed a few days convalescence.

Richard Hayes Harland was discharged after his second injury, which was a relief for Annie, his wife of only two years. Mrs Sale who lived on Church Road was aware that her husband, Albert, had been killed the previous year in France. Mr Herbert Hunter, whose family resided at 'Ashville' in Loring Road, had been promoted to Captain of his regiment.

Mrs Henrietta Meeham from Raven Hall, had recently been fined one pound for shining a lamp during the blackout. She was part of a group who were gathering pieces of wool from fences and hedgerows. When sufficient had been accumulated to fill a large sack, it was sent to the national collection point in London, and was eventually woven into warm blankets for injured servicemen.

Above: Mrs Wrightson on back row with soldiers on leave.

Above: Vi and children with chickens before Pollard Cottage was built.

Below: A visitor arrives at the farm showing St. Hilda's in the background

The hard-working eleven-year-old Billy Stubbs, eagerly joined them in this most worthwhile cause. He also picked heather to be distributed among the soldiers at Liverpool Infirmary. Billy was so full of energy that he also worked on Jonty Robinson's farm at weekends and during school holidays.

A sports day at which all residents of Ravenscar, Staintondale and Howdale were welcome, was held at Church Farm. Prizes for the children's races were porridge plates, milk goblets, crayons, pens and pencils. Ladies won either a cream jug and sugar basin or a china dish: the winning gentlemen were given penknives or silk handkerchiefs.

The Robinson family with Hannah Lightfoot, Billy Stubbs and Belgian lady

Fresh news arrived from abroad - the Beeforths had really been 'In the wars'. Tom Beeforth was in Alexandria suffering from malaria, while Joseph in France had a wounded foot. Harold Ward of 'Bay View Villa', was also in France, fit and well, after recovering from a bout of flu.

Eighteen months after Ruby Miles had left Mill Farm, the announcement of her death from pneumonia came as a major shock to past friends. Miss Dalkin and Johnson Robinson, travelled by train to Scalby, where his brother Harold was waiting with the pony and trap. On route to the funeral at Langdale End, they passed Hackness Church where Vi and Jonty had married. Approaching their destination, he looked across to the fields he had once ploughed and sowed in his youth.

When the service was over he took the opportunity to call on his mother for tea before they journeyed home. A headstone in Langdale End churchyard reads 'In loving memory of Ruby daughter of R. W. and E. J. Miles. 1892 – 1918 Thy Will Be Done.'

Ruby Miles' headstone

Each individual in their own way came to terms with the aftermath of war, when it finally ended on the eleventh hour of the eleventh day of the eleventh month of 1918. Classes were held to discuss the problems of construction, following the war. *'Subjects debated were 'The principle of the minimum wage' and 'Can the U.K., by improved methods of agriculture, support itself in food production?"*

Fundraising for the chancel continued with an evening based on Charles Dickens' 'A Christmas Carol', presented by Mr Carter, who, with his usual theatrical gusto brought each character to life. Magic Lantern slides accompanied the recitation and were shown by Mr F. Dalby Bulmer.

The new year of 1919 brought with it relief and hope from four terrible years of conflict and death. Frank Wrightson from Ravenscar House was home on a month's leave and due to return to civilian life very soon. Mrs Emily Duck of Crag Farm was overjoyed to see her sons William and Tom - as were the families of Privates F.W. Wedgwood, W. Reynolds, G. Pickering, Bombardier H. Porter and seaman J.W. Coultas. John Micklethwaite had recovered from being gassed, and James Sharp was granted two months' leave after being a prisoner of war. By February, Edwin Duck, William Duck and Edgar Ward had been demobbed.

World War 1 gas mask

A family from Doncaster, Mr and Mrs Brewer, along with daughters Gertrude and Constance, had been enjoying holidays and weekends in Loring Road where they occupied the house next to the railway crossing. Sadly, in 1919 they were grief-stricken by the loss of their eldest daughter Gertrude, who was buried near the entrance to the church.

Mr and Mrs Thompson (not to be confused with Mr Thompson the grocer) moved from Wykeham to Springfield Farm in April 1919. On the morning of the 27th they awoke to twelve inches of snow and must have asked themselves, 'why have we moved here?' Fortunately, the next day the warmth from the bright sunshine quickly melted the unwelcomed snow. Vi Robinson had known Mr Thompson from her earlier years at Hackness when he had travelled round their village selling groceries and sweets.

Peace celebrations were organised jointly between Ravenscar and Staintondale. Ravenscar children started the programme by plaiting ribbons as they danced round the Maypole. This was followed by a fancy dress parade and sports events, which culminated with Staintondale overpowering Ravenscar in a tug of war competition. Staintondale children then performed a pageant featuring 'Father Time', 'The Seasons' and 'The Months', before tea was served. Each child was presented with a peace mug and the festivities came to a climax with splendid fireworks.

Mr Carter's drawing room with pianola and pictures of sailing ships

One October morning, in gale-force winds, Mr Carter noticed a majestic five-masted sailing ship ashore at Stoupe

Beck. Apparently, it had been en route to Hartlepool for repairs and had parted company with the tugs. Next day when the wind abated, Mr Carter, a yachting enthusiast, was keen to take a closer look at the stranded schooner. He went equipped with camera and was accompanied by his wife Amy, and young Jack Green, as they too would be interested, having travelled with him on his yacht. Mr Carter's drawing room reflected his sailing and musical interests.

Stranded 'Cap Palos' with Mrs Carter and Jack Green looking on, taken by Sydney Carter

Heavy rain and snow hit this area at the time peace was declared. On Tuesday the 11th of November everything was a white-out for Armistice Day. The church bell was rung prior to 11 o'clock, when a two minute silence was observed all over Britain to remember those who had laid down their lives. People were feeling uplifted and secure following the end of hostilities. Within days, Vi's sister Lily arrived for a week's holiday and Mrs Carter sent pretty cards to the village children inviting them to a special party at Crag Hill. Lily noted in her diary *'So sorry Hannah is leaving Vi's next week after three years. Such a dear girl, so willing to do anything. So respectful and so kind with the children'.*

Gradually, one by one, the soldiers returned and found employment at the brickworks or on the railway. Others chose to be agricultural labourers or joined the recently opened ganister quarry, on the moor between Ravenscar and the Whitby to Scarborough road. Once again enjoying family life, they would look forward to a traditional Christmas. The Church was elaborately decorated ready for the Sunday School party. In a corner of the Institute room, a large fir tree was adorned with many presents that caused its branches to droop under the weight. Excited children eagerly awaited Santa Claus; this privilege was bestowed on Mr Reynolds who with a beaming smile, distributed the gifts to them.

Noel Wrightson collected a special prize for having the highest marks at Sunday School.

Sadly, for some households there would still be an empty place at the table. A memorial in the church reads:

'To the glory of God and in honoured memory of the men from the parish of Ravenscar who fell in the war 1914 – 1918.'

H. Bennett. W. Cooper. W.K. Duck. G. Harland.
T. Headlam. H.S. Jacques. J. Massheder. T. Mennell.
G. Pickering. J.W. Pressick. J.H. Robinson. A.V. Sale.
J. Sayers. R.J. Vaughan. S.S. Waddington.

'Live thou for England – We for England died.'

***

CHAPTER FIVE

NORMALITY RETURNS

With a new decade and hope for long lasting peace, a more relaxed atmosphere descended on the village.

Before the children returned to school after the Christmas break, Miss Dalkin decided to throw open the doors of her home to all the pupils and give them afternoon tea, provided by her sister Miss Mary Ann Dalkin. Afterwards, to continue the New Year celebrations, they walked to the schoolroom where parents joined them for games and dancing. In class Miss Dalkin was noted for her strictness; rules were not put in place to be broken. When scholars arrived late they recall having to knock in order to gain entry, as the doors were locked at nine o'clock prompt! This popular teacher was also remembered as a very kind lady with a jovial sense of humour that came to the fore in her school concert productions.

Competitive team games were re-established. Ravenscar and Staintondale Football Club held regular Saturday matches throughout the winter. In May, the Staintondale and Ravenscar Cricket Club took to the field; although both cricket and football teams were often on the losing side their enthusiasm never wavered.

During the summer months, agricultural shows in the surrounding districts sprung to life and once again farmers could parade their animals hoping to come away with a first prize. In the horticultural section, keen gardeners gained great satisfaction by producing winning home-grown vegetables and flowers.

A pleasant surprise was in store for the Sunday School children, when money from the annual church bazaar was earmarked to pay for an outing to Whitby to explore its winding streets; its quaint shops; the harbour and the famous ruined Abbey, before enjoying a special afternoon picnic. Only a few days prior to this on August 16th 1920, a sunny breezy day, Vi, Jonty, and several others boarded the nine thirty train for Whitby to witness the awe inspiring sight of sailing ships at the regatta, made all the more enjoyable by the favourable weather conditions.

The building of a new vicarage on School Lane never materialized, not even a turf was removed. The Ecclesiastical Commissioners must have been overjoyed when Mr Carter, the Vicar's Warden, offered to sell them his property 'Corbie'. As from September 16th 1920, the date of a conveyance between the two parties, the Rev. Clark and any future vicar would enjoy living in this well-appointed vicarage on the Esplanade.

Local agricultural labourers, who were at home having their compulsory annual holidays, during the quiet time in the farming calendar, were able to enjoy the Martinmas social evening at the Church Rooms. These farm workers known as 'Martmas Lads' were given a twelve-month contract and taken on as a first wagoner, second wagoner, or as a plough lad. Every year farmers hiring new hands, and young men in need of work, would congregate at the George Hotel, Scarborough where new contracts were agreed for the following year.

Christmas was looming and for the fourth successive year Vi, along with her cherubs, an affectionate name used by their favourite Aunt, went to see Santa Claus at the 'Rem' (The Remnant Warehouse), better known as Boyes store. Children not fortunate enough to visit him there, had the opportunity to meet him in the Church Rooms at the Sunday School Christmas party. So crowded was the room that tea was served at three sittings. That year, Mr Robinson, 'Jonty', took on the role of Santa Claus using a pillow case for the gifts, as he would do at home. With four of his own children among a group of sixty excited youngsters, it must have been difficult to hide his true identity.

A portable harmonium, which would be useful for choir practices, was presented to the Church in memory of Agnes de Selincourt who had resided at 'Thistledown' (Cliff House) for three years until her death at Whitby in 1917. Her executors sold the house to Mrs Agnes Wheatley in 1920. The

Rev. Arthur M. Bury and his wife who had recently moved from Skelton would be very grateful for this latest gift.

The Clough family, also recent arrivals to the village, opened a drapery business and the following advertisement ran for several months in the Scarborough Mercury:-

> **'RAVENSCAR DRAPERY AND BOOT WAREHOUSE.**
> **Proprietor: Barker, Clough & Co.**
> *The House for quality and reasonable prices, has an excellent selection of the following goods; Blankets, Sheets, Down Quilts, White and Fancy Table Covers, Bolster and Pillowcases, Combs., Vests, Bodices, Spencers, Corsets, Shirts, Socks, Pants, Stockings, Flannelette Prints, Tabralco, Towels, Towelling, Casement Cloths, etc.*
>
> *A Fine assortment of Crepe-de-Chine, Luvisca, Georgette, Hercules and other Blouses.*
>
> *LADIES' HEAVY WINTER COATS, from £3 17s. 6d. Our representative will be pleased to call upon you at any time with samples on receipt of postcard. All goods on approval and carriage paid. Money returned if not satisfied.'*

Mrs Clough, née Barker, was an active member of the Church and her daughter Leila joined in concerts and fancy dress events.

In the early twenties several other new families arrived in the area. A new stationmaster, Mr Leake, who took on the position of church organist, moved into Station House with his wife and children, Ivy, Olive and Stanley. Mr and Mrs Acomb and children went to 'Ranworth' followed by Mr and Mrs France's family who moved next door to 'Ravenhurst'- these two semi-detached houses had previously been known as 'Church Villas'. Mr Brown with his wife Nurse Brown, the local midwife, lived at 'The White House'. Other arrivals were the Birdsall family from Skewsby. Unfortunately, their intended destination, 'Rudda Farm', owned by Mr Micklethwaite was not ready for occupation, and temporarily they were accommodated at nearby Moorland House with the Monkman family.

The village was lucky to have fine weather on September 28th 1921, when the Institute was opened by Mr Andrews of Cloughton; the next day was an absolute 'pea-souper'. During the course of the day's merrymaking, Mr Carter and the Vicar also made speeches. Lily, determined not to miss the event, push-biked from Hackness, her cycle basket overflowing with flowers for the table vases. Meanwhile the ladies of the village artistically arranged a selection of sandwiches, fancy buns and cakes. A decorated commemoration cake formed the centre piece and Lily's contribution of fresh flowers added the final touches to a wonderful display. One lady wrote *'The hut was beautifully finished off; white enamel inside and cement outside'.* A whist drive and dance brought the celebrations to an end, but the dance would have been more pleasurable if it had not been overcrowded. The building had cost in the region of £1000, and both the architect, Mr Rickinson, and the builders, Skelton & Sons, were from Robin Hood's Bay. There was now a marked increase in social activities, as functions were arranged at every opportunity, in an attempt to reduce the debt on the building.

The Men's Club, booked every Monday and Thursday evenings, where members enjoyed playing dominoes, snooker, darts and card games. Mr Reynolds organised a fancy dress ball at Christmas when sixty adults and children arrived in costume. Due to its success this event became an annual occasion, as did the New Year's fancy dress party arranged by the Folk Dancing Club. Mr Carter continued with his highly entertaining lantern lectures, and Mr Thompson (known to his close friends as 'Pal') of Springfield Farm arranged a visit from some top class Scarborough artistes. After staging a very polished performance they were thanked by Mr Carter who with his usual humorous comments, compared the concert party *'to a band of explorers discovering a 'terra incognito' hitherto regarded as uninhabited'*

Mrs Bury's 1922 production of 'Aladdin'
Those identified are, on front row, left to right;-
1.Madge Lazenby; 3.Peggy Lazenby; 4. Mary Wedgwood;
5. Bessie Robinson; 6. Nellie Lightfoot.

Mrs Bury's theatrical prowess shone through as she directed a brilliant performance of the Arabian Nights story of 'Aladdin'. This would be the first of many in aid of the Church of England Society for Waifs and Strays. Dazzling costumes were made by Mrs Carter who excelled with needle and thread. The outcome was a production to rival anything staged professionally. Subsequently with her immense flair she directed other children's plays including: 'Babes in the Wood' and 'Red Riding Hood'. An unusual pairing of two stories, namely 'Snow White and the Seven Dwarfs' and 'Goldilocks and The Three Bears' were moulded together and the play became 'Snow White and the Three Bears'. A newspaper report praised this production:

'The children's efforts were loudly applauded by a large audience and the scenery and dresses were greatly admired. The part of 'Snow White' was very prettily played by Mary Wrightson, Lucy Thompson looked fine as the wicked 'Queen

Myra', Mary Wedgwood and Madge Lazenby were excellent as 'Katy and Aunt Maude'.

Ivy Leake made a dainty little 'Fairy Queen'. 'The Three Bears', played by Jack Green, Noel Wrightson and Ronald Marples caused great amusement. Margaret Lancaster acted capitally as the 'Lord Chamberlain' and Leslie Carter looked a thorough little 'Prince''.

On a pre-arranged date, one unfortunate lady had all her teeth extracted, when both the dentist and doctor could be present. Ether had been administered as the anaesthetic. For several days she suffered with pain and felt exhausted, but neighbours rallied round. Mrs Acomb looked after the children during the daytime whilst Mrs Ward took care of washing and ironing. This was a prime example of community spirit in the village.

Staintondale and Ravenscar Cricket Club held a whist drive and dance in the schoolroom at Staintondale. As the captain's wife, Mrs Johnson Robinson was asked to present the prizes. Mr Robinson, who took on the captaincy in 1917, was looking forward to his fifth season at the helm. Mr Wilson accompanied the dancing at the piano loaned by Mr Cross of Bell Hill Farm. A year later, before the start of the 1922 cricket season; the club decided to have a friendly game on May 13th, when Ravenscar played Staintondale on their home ground adjacent to the Shepherd's Arms. The two teams were as follows:

Ravenscar: J. Thompson. F. Wrightson. J. Brown. C. Wrightson. J. Robinson. R. Price. T. Acomb. W. Lloyd. T. Wrightson. H. Thompson. F. Green.

Staintondale: W. Leonard. W. Cross. H. Lyon. G. Pressick. F. Kendall. C. Wilson. G. Lyon. W. Hall. J. Goodall. T. Masterman. T. Leonard.

Ravenscar won by two runs. J. Robinson took six wickets and the highest scorer was H. Lyon with twenty four runs. The joint club had their final season together in 1923 before Ravenscar decided to start its own club. In January 1924 a report stated: - *'A new Cricket Club has been formed at Ravenscar, and the ground is just behind the Memorial Hall, three minutes from the station. This is now being levelled in preparation for the coming season'.* Mr Acomb was appointed as secretary. At this point, dear reader, I should point out that the Memorial Hall and Recreation Hall were one and the same.

The new Ravenscar cricket team

Back row, left to right: F. Robinson; F. Wrightson; W. Goforth (Umpire); F. Sanders; Mr Pickering (Scorer); T. Masterman; W. Hodgson; Front row: T. Lightfoot; T. Acomb; W. Lloyd; R. France; J. Robinson; Sitting in front: G. Stanforth.

Parishioners of St Hilda's Church saw the completion of their new chancel in 1923, which was dedicated by the Archbishop of York on June 4th. The cornerstone had been laid a year earlier by the Bishop of Hull. Building was undertaken by Skelton Bros. from Robin Hood's Bay, the same firm that had constructed the Recreation Hall. Two Scarborough men, Mr Welford and Mr Lancaster also worked on the chancel and lodged at Church Farm. During the summer of the same year Mrs Jackson decided to retire as the sub-postmistress. The Post Office moved into new premises at the grocer's shop in Station Square, which was run by the Thompson family.

Building of the new chancel at St Hilda's, Ravenscar

Fancy dress parade at Raven Hall

This year on August Bank Holiday Monday, the residents had a sports day and carnival all rolled into one event. Proceedings began with a fancy dress parade that set out from Station Square and made its way to the Raven Hall Hotel. A lovely fine day resulted in a large number of entries, and at its destination the procession was welcomed by an enthusiastic crowd of locals and holidaymakers. Prize winners were: Children: John Acomb, 'Cupid'; Leslie Carter, 'Japanese Girl'; and Ronnie Marples, 'Nestles'. Ladies: Miss Harrison, 'Indian Girl'; Miss M. Lazenby, 'Cowboy'; and Miss L. Thompson, 'Flower Girl'. Men: J. Green, 'Donoghue'; and W. Lloyd, 'Clown'. The procession was joined by Cloughton Brass Band as they made their way to the Recreation Hall and the sports were held in Mr Thompson's field. Everyone participated in the usual races, but extra events included throwing the cricket ball, pole jumping, a bending bicycle race, a half mile pony race, and potato race. The sports were followed in the evening with a dance and music provided by Mr Clark playing violin, accompanied on the piano by Mr Allanson.

The Robinson children at Church Farm
Left to right: John, Jim, Harry, Ann, Bessie, with Alice in front.

In the New Year of 1924 the majority of children in the village were struck down with whooping cough. The worst affected were taken down to the brickworks to inhale the steam from the boiler room, as they believed it would ease the symptoms of this terrible infection. Fortunately, by mid-January the children had improved sufficiently to attend dancing lessons with Mr Carter at Crag Hill in preparation for another performance organised by Mrs Bury.

Back to life on the land, Jonty's older children realised that living on a farm involved hard work. The girls delivered milk in enamel cans to nearby houses and also churned the butter. By the age of five they were expected to help with potato picking, and at seven, two of them were tending cows on the roadside, keeping an eye on the animals grazing between the church and mill corner. When Harry was old enough to take his turn, he would gather bunches of violets for Miss Goforth who lived at Mill Farm and in return would be rewarded with a handful of sweets. This lady, a seamstress, was kept very busy with repairs and making delightful dresses for the local children. Vi was also productive 'buttering up' using her pats and decorative roller. The end product was in demand both in Ravenscar and Scarborough. Mr Sedman, a butcher from Burniston, who delivered meat every Friday by horse and cart would take as much butter as Vi could spare.

Cows with village school in the background

Her daughter Ann recalls seeing weighing scales in the rear of the cart with spikes on the pan to hold the meat in place. Mr Wallis from Rowntrees the grocers in Scarborough, delivered provisions that were not readily available at the village shop.

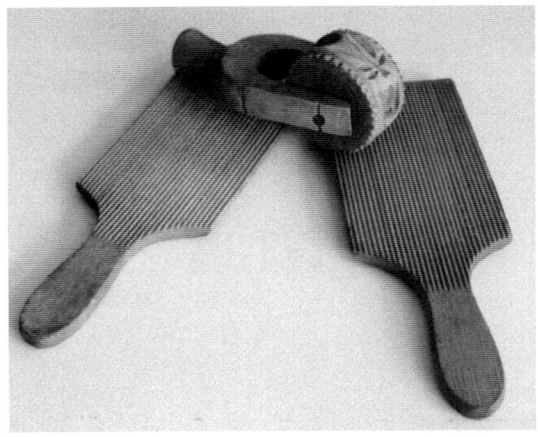

Left: Butter pats with decorative roller

Right: Mr Sedman on his rounds.

The parishioners said goodbye to their popular vicar and his wife, Mrs Bury who had been responsible for organising dramatic children's plays. It was time for them to move on to pastures new. Rev. Bury's new congregation at Wykeham soon realised what a blessing this couple were to their village. At the same time Miss Dalkin retired as headmistress, and as a parting gift presented the school with a set of community song books. She was replaced by Mrs Atkin from Scarborough who travelled daily by train with her son Billy. The truant inspector, Mr Dobinson would patrol local villages on the lookout for children avoiding school. When they heard the humming sound of his motorbike they shouted "It's the kiddycatcher!" before running for cover.

Christmas party for local children at Raven Hall Hotel

On the 11th March 1927, the local paper reported that:
'A protection order was granted in respect of the temporary transfer of the Raven Hall Hotel Ravenscar from Mr Fred Pacey to Sydney Hammond Carter ....Mr Westrope, of Messrs

Birdsall & Cross, who made the application, said it was desired to transfer the licence temporarily to Mr Carter, as secretary of the Company. Mr Carter was resident at Ravenscar and had on a previous occasion held the licence.'

Above: Photograph presented by Mr Dobinson to 100% attendees at school in 1926

Below: Jim Robinson collecting coal aged 8

Above: Publicity photograph of gentleman with Morris saloon at Raven Hall Hotel,
Below: The dining room at Raven Hall Hotel

Mr Wrightson's son Clive successfully passed the Board of Trade examination as second mate in March 1927. Sadly the following year this young man contracted a serious disease abroad and later died in Middlesbrough Infirmary. He is buried in Ravenscar churchyard.

Above: Rev. and Mrs Bury outside Ravenscar Church

Yet another lady, who contributed so much to the social life in Ravenscar and was held in high esteem by all who knew her, died only three years after leaving the village. Mrs Bury, the wife of the Rev A.M. Bury, who was then the Vicar of Wykeham, was killed in a car accident on 16th September 1928. While on holiday with her sister in Lincolnshire, their car veered off the road near Grantham. Her sister was also injured. From the time Mrs Bury had moved to Wykeham the locals had missed her annual fairy plays and when another similar event was announced over a hundred people were in the audience to watch a programme of songs, recitals, dances, sketches and plays. The highlight of the evening was a combination of stories in one play entitled 'Revels in Dreamland' written by Miss Constance Lancaster. Only three performers in the cast were above twelve years old. The evening was so successful that it was repeated the following Monday.

St Hilda's Church Ravenscar, Parochial Church Council. Top row from left: Mr Thompson (farmer); Miss Dalkin (schoolmistress); G.D.Birdsall. Front row: C. Wrightson; Rev. A.M. Bury; Mrs Bury; Miss Dalkin (sister of teacher); Mr Thompson (grocer).

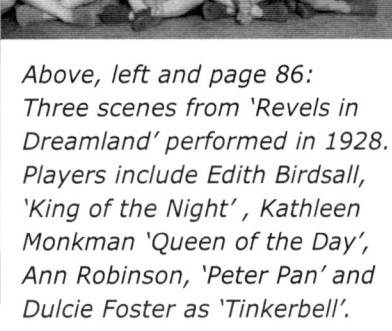

Above, left and page 86: Three scenes from 'Revels in Dreamland' performed in 1928. Players include Edith Birdsall, 'King of the Night', Kathleen Monkman 'Queen of the Day', Ann Robinson, 'Peter Pan' and Dulcie Foster as 'Tinkerbell'.

One day Mrs Carter surprised Mrs Atkin and her pupils by presenting them with two stuffed animals, a snarling badger and a cute little vixen.

That year a Women's Institute was formed and monthly meetings were held in the Memorial Hall. Mrs T. Thompson of Station Square was appointed President, Mrs Marples of 'Ashville', Loring Road, Secretary, and Mrs T. White from Bent Rigg Farm, Treasurer. Amongst other founder members were Mrs Acomb, 'Ranworth', Mrs France, 'Ravenhurst' and Mrs J. Robinson, Church Farm.

At Crag Hill, Mr Carter's nieces and nephews regularly stayed with them in the school holidays. Looking back, Oliver Lancaster was surprised how much time his uncle Sydney Carter devoted to helping him build a model yacht.

'No effort spared, we even melted down some lead piping on a Primus stove to make the keel. On completion and in uncle's absence I was desperate to try it out. There being no suitable ponds in Ravenscar, undeterred I tucked it under my arm and went down to the sea ,where I launched it in an off-shore breeze and watched her bravely set a course for Denmark,

never to be seen again. I don't think she had even been given a name, but perhaps 'Marie Celeste' would have been appropriate. When Uncle returned and I had to tell him the sad news. Instead of telling me how stupid I had been and losing all interest in me, he went to Pickering, to a professional model-maker, and bought a beautiful model with the name 'Viking', which I still possess'.

Ravenscar tunnel attracted curious youngsters. Bessie Robinson had been told by the Stationmaster's daughter that Sunday was a good day to explore it as no trains would be running. After Sunday School she persuaded her two younger brothers John and Jim to join her on this adventure. Walking into the dark void would no doubt be a scary experience, but eventually a small shaft of light appeared at the far entrance, which became much larger as their goal was almost accomplished. Climbing the grass-covered bank side they suddenly heard a rumbling sound coming from the tunnel, which increased dramatically until a special Sunday excursion train emerged from the entrance and rushed by en route to Robin Hood's Bay. Three very lucky children indeed!

A year or so later, two young boys, Oliver Lancaster and Stanley Leake, the Stationmaster's son, went on the same escapade. They selected a time when no trains were scheduled for a few hours. About a hundred and fifty yards into the tunnel, to their horror, they heard a loud puffing noise and toot on the whistle, the familiar sound of a train approaching from the brickyard. Oliver gives a very detailed account of what happened next.

'Panic stricken, we turned and ran back, but it was obvious we would not get out in time, so we dashed into a little 'refuge' in the side of the tunnel, presumably provided for this purpose! We covered our ears with our hands as it roared past emitting exceedingly nasty acrid smoke, and after it had passed, we lost no time in getting out again, to find that we both had black faces! When running into the 'refuge' we had put our outspread hands on the wet sooty wall, before covering our ears. At this time there were still some patches of snow lying about, and we did our best to use this to try to clean ourselves up. We never

told anyone about our adventure, and it had been an extraordinary chance that we had just picked a time when a relatively un-scheduled train was due.'

Jack Green, encouraged to study music by Mr Carter, started to play the bugle and later progressed to the cornet and trumpet. After some time when he was more proficient, he would load the Weber pianola with rolls that he could play along to. Mr Carter paid for him to have professional lessons at the Londesborough Theatre Scarborough where his teacher was the lead trumpet player in the orchestra from the Capitol Picture House. The Scarborough Mercury reported:

'This super cinema was well received as a valuable addition to the entertainment facilities in the town when it opened on March 11th 1929. Its facade was built of white glazed faience and with simple classical ornamentation gave a striking appearance to theatre goers. The auditorium was lavishly decorated to give the effect of a large drawing room. It seated two thousand one hundred patrons with circle balcony and stalls. Extra width between rows gave the public a feeling of relaxed comfort'.

A grand organ built by Fitton and Hayley from Leeds was installed. It consisted of two manuals and pedal board. There were twenty seven ranks of pipes which were of orchestral variety, plus tonal percussions including chimes and glockenspiel along with thirty special effects, which included a siren, telephone bell, dog bark, police whistle, thunder roll, and aeroplane. Mr J.W. Ainsworth who played for many years in Bradford was the organist. A full orchestra was also employed led by Walter Paynter who came from the St Georges Hall in Bradford. Sydney Carter, a main director of the company was responsible for this super palace of entertainment. Jack Green's musicianship went from strength to strength; he played with the orchestra in 'The Gondoliers' at the Opera House in St Thomas Street. His biggest achievement was to play with the Scarborough Symphony Orchestra at the famous Grand Hotel.

The same year the local football team nicknamed 'The Dales' had a better season and made it through to the semi-finals of both the Scarborough Hospital Cup and the District Cup. The villagers were passionate about sport, consequently a Hockey Club was formed with six-a-side practices on Saturdays. Tom White was considered to be one of the strongest players. The Men's Club held a military whist drive and dance and invited members of the Women's Institute to their special social evening. Dancing till midnight was accompanied by an electric gramophone, a new invention at the time.

The Folk Dancing Club held a fundraising event to pay for their travelling expenses to a tournament at Castle Howard. Those who took part in the singing were Mrs Birdsall, Mrs T. Thompson, and Miss A. Jackson. Mr J. Green gave an excellent cornet solo and the evening finished with folk and sword dancing. The day proved to be a huge success, both mixed and ladies' teams gained second place in their relevant classes.

Ravenscar schoolchildren did their village proud in a national competition. John Robinson aged thirteen years of Church Farm won five shillings in a drawing and painting competition. John Acomb of 'Ranworth' won a prize in the same category and Maggie Ward aged ten of 'Bay View' collected a book prize in an English literature competition.

Miss Dalkin's farewell to her friends in Ravenscar

Two sisters revered by all and who played a large part in the social life, prepared to leave their friends and return north to Croft-on-Tees, near where they had come from fifteen years earlier. Miss Dalkin had been head teacher for about thirteen years before taking retirement in 1925. Miss Mary Ann Dalkin had assisted Mrs Carter with producing some wonderful costumes for the plays and concerts featured in this glorious decade of the twenties.

The Dalkin sisters in retirement

CHAPTER SIX

THE CHANGING THIRTIES

To celebrate the beginning of a new decade, the ladies of the Women's Institute decided to invite the members of the Men's Club to their annual New Year's Party reciprocating the gesture of the recent Christmas gathering. Games included 'Musical Consequences', 'The Tinga Linga Lary Man' and 'John Brown's Baby'. Goodness knows how they played them! Dances were held on a regular basis with either George Wedgwood or Gowan Pickering playing the melodeon; or they really 'pushed the boat out' by booking the Magnet Dance Band. One lady told me "we had some good 'hops' in those days". The Institute continued with monthly meetings and guest speakers came to talk on various industrious subjects connected with everyday household economics. Demonstrations included cookery tips, glove and rug making along with cake decorating.

The cigarette dispenser on Church Farm wall, with young Geoff White and his relatives.

At one meeting, William Lloyd who successfully exhibited poultry, was asked to judge the best dressed fowl along with a plate of six eggs, regarding the latter, uniformity of size and colour would determine the winner.

William lived at the lodge with his parents; his father Alfred was the postman for many years whilst his mother sold sweets and tobacco. It must have been good business as Mr Thompson from Station Square regularly filled up the dispensing machine on the barn door at Church Farm. The dispenser held packets of woodbines, an inexpensive cigarette at the time.

Elsewhere in the country millions of people experienced difficulties with the tightening grip of the depression. Men were without jobs and even with their dole money, struggled to put food on the table. At least in Ravenscar, people found things a little easier and three people I know of bred chickens: Mr Pyne at Moorfield Farm, Mr Acomb and Mr Lloyd. Almost everybody grew their own vegetables, plus there was a plentiful supply of milk. Rabbit and pigeon shooting days were very popular and provided succulent pies and stews.

At Church Farm, Mr Robinson's family were growing up and realising just how strenuous farm life could be. This would entail working long hours seven days a week. John the eldest son (my father) had left school. The opportunity of taking on extra land from Mr Lotherington came just at the right time: twenty-six acres of rough grazing surrounded by woodland, and situated a mile south of the mill on the Staintondale Road, gave excellent shelter for the bullocks and heifers.

A local fisherman, Tom Shippey, decided to settle in Loring Road, Ravenscar and brought his small coble on to the rocks beneath the 9-hole golf course built at Raven Hall during the early twenties. He would row excited teenagers frequently to Robin Hood's Bay and back. When his fishing nets needed repairing, he would haul them up the steep path to his home, fastening one end of the net to the station crossing gate and the other to his own. A local villager sold the catch from a wicker basket around the community; many looked forward to this treat. One day a local lad came upon her slumped against a wall. He enquired, "Do you need any help?" She replied, "Nay lad, get yer sen yam, it's Mr Lightfoot's mead that's done this t' me".

Above: Tom Shippey and his boat with visitors
Below: Raven Hall Golf Course

Ravenscar was known to lie on a fault and during the early thirties a substantial earth tremor caused a crack to appear on a track above the old Alum Works. One witness said it was wide enough to fit a foot in. John Robinson's cast iron bed travelled across the bedroom floor and at 'Rigg Hall' where Mary Consitt (my mother) lived, ornaments rattled on the shelves.

George Lightfoot who was categorised as a master builder had recently built a property for himself in School Lane known as 'Fairview'. This detached house was constructed of stone removed from a derelict property at the old Alum Works. His next project was to build two further detached properties along Pollard Road; the first to be erected was 'Broom Rise' and the second, 'Gorse Cottage'. George owned an early battery powered radio which was his constant companion during his building work. My father, with a carthorse and flat lorry, helped transport some of the stone, which was quarried by Willie Binns and Tom Duck. George's masonry skills are still to be seen today as a testament to his craftsmanship.

George Lightfoot pictured in the 1950s

Willie Binns & Tom Duck working at the quarry

Above: Building the foundations of Broom Rise
Below: Having a tea break on the roof of Broom Rise

J.B. Priestley, the well-known author, decided to take a restful break, and chose the peaceful setting of the Raven Hall Hotel. No doubt he would need solitary space to recharge his batteries after the successful launch of his novel 'The Good Companions'. Did he know the owner Mr Sydney Carter? Or was it pure coincidence that they were both Bradfordians? Sydney, at this time was also president of the Scarborough Amateur Operatic Society and had triumphed playing the Lord Chancellor in Gilbert and Sullivan's comic opera 'Iolanthe' at the Opera House in St Thomas Street. A later production, 'Pirates of Penzance,' brought a capacity audience, and in his address to the company, Mr Carter said, *"in this age of machinery when commercialism was driving out legitimate theatre, it was left to amateurs to keep alive those immortal works which were the result of the wonderful combination of Gilbert and Sullivan".*

Sydney Carter playing the Lord Chancellor in Gilbert & Sullivan's 'Iolanthe'

Meanwhile Scarborough had ambitious plans drawn up for the Open Air Theatre where the Amateur Operatic Society was involved in productions of popular musical shows. Mr Carter was very much at the forefront of this operation, which culminated in the first ever showing in 1932 of 'Merrie England' by Edward German. In stark contrast, it was a very sad time at Crag Hill as Mrs Carter had recently passed away. Around this period he presented the church with a fine reredos to stand behind the altar; his generosity to the church was never ending. He had also decided to sell the Raven Hall Hotel to Mr J.R. Cooper, and within two years he would leave Crag Hill with its beautiful landscaped garden, which had been his home for over twenty years. The following could have been his very last advert in the local paper of May 23rd 1931.

SPEND SUNDAY AT THE RAVEN HALL HOTEL
THE RAVEN HALL ORCHESTRA will play in the Lounge for Afternoon Tea and Dinner.
THE GOLF COURSE is open to Visitors. Green Fees 2/6 day
Special Inclusive Week-end Terms during May and June

A few months prior to this an application for a licence extension over the Christmas period had been refused on the grounds that it would be necessary to have a policeman on duty as it may attract undesirables.

His new abode was in Scarborough, and chauffeur Dick Reynolds followed him leaving his semi-detached house in Church Road. The new occupier of Crag Hill, Mrs Morris, ran the property as a private hotel.

Youngsters wandering round the old alum quarry looking for fossils or perhaps picking brambles could not resist attempting to run up the steep shale hillside to the three brick archways (I've never heard of anyone achieving this feat). These were eventually blown up by the Army during the war. The young girls could also be mischievous, on more than one occasion Mr Blakely of Cliff House found his cabbages had been sheared off and spiked on his sundial. They also crept under a wire fence near the hotel vegetable garden to investigate the wishing well below the terraced gardens. Often these capers were after Sunday School.

Under the supervision of an official coastguard, frequent practices were held and the rescue equipment was left permanently loaded on a sledge or cart, ready to be yoked up for transporting to the rocket post. The hawser, breeches buoy and tripod were all assembled by the auxiliaries, Mr Wrightson being one of them. In the summer months sightseers would congregate near the cliff to witness this complicated procedure. Nearby on these balmy warm days Mrs Wrightson would be serving teas to the visitors on the grass between Ravenscar House and the Vicarage.

Equipment loaded for breeches buoy rescue

Charles Wrightson stabilising the tripod

Above: The breeches buoy being winched up the cliff

Below: Tea party for viewers of the breeches buoy practice

On Christmas Day 1932, King George V made the very first Royal broadcast to the nation. Only a handful of local people would possess a radio, so no doubt Mr Lightfoot had a capacity audience in his front room for this momentous occasion in history, which became an annual event even to this day.

As the years went by the villagers, enjoyed participating in even more team competitions: tennis, cricket, football, hockey and sword and folk dancing. The dancers took part in annual contests, firstly at Castle Howard and later at Mulgrave Castle near Whitby. The six-man team of sword dancers was coached by Billy Stubbs with Tom and Ted Duck, Oliver Lancaster, Stanley Leake, Billy Atkins and Stephen Birdsall. The folk dancing team entered a competition at Mulgrave Castle. One dance was entitled 'The Goddesses', in which the team danced in pairs: Alice Robinson and Tom Duck, Winnie Temple and Stephen Birdsall, Mabel France and John Acomb, plus the final pair, Harry Robinson and Gladys Cross. One of my sources recalls practising at Raven Hall; they sported large pink plaits in their hair to replicate a horse's mane. The schoolmistress encouraged her pupils to enter a variety of competitions (as referred to in the last chapter). Now it was the time for nine year old Ted Duck to bring honour to the small school which only mustered about twenty attendees. At the Eskdale Tournament of Song at Whitby, he was awarded first prize in the junior class for elocution and was presented with a silver cup. Between the ages of twelve and fourteen, youngsters had the opportunity to attend woodwork or cookery lessons at Scalby. They caught the nine o'clock train and walked from the station through Scalby Village, passing St. Laurence's Church and down to the school.

Back in Ravenscar an educational trip was arranged to see the ganister railway which was a short walk from the school. Ganister was a silicon-rich rock used in the lining of furnaces and in the manufacture of fire bricks. As they watched the wagons travelling up and down the bank side, an empty ascending truck mysteriously came off the rails. A young girl was hit and received heavy bruising and grazing to her arm.

In today's world, health and safety would have had a field day!

Above: Schoolchildren c. 1933

Below: Stanley Leake on horseback with Charles Wrightson

The county library books held at the school were exchanged weekly after school hours on Wednesdays, and by the spring of 1933 Mrs Acomb housed the library at 'Ranworth'. This year the shortage of water was even more serious than in the Autumn of 1929, when Church Farm was rationed to drawing water for one hour per day; now it was a case of carrying buckets of water from Mr Duck's well at Crag Hill Farm. On both occasions the reservoirs were completely dry. At the church service held on Rogation Sunday, the Rev. Norman Cox asked all his parishioners to pray for rain and to continue to do so in their daily prayers.

Miss Steele, the new schoolmistress who had taken over the post from Mrs Atkin, travelled daily by train from Robin Hood's Bay. A dedicated teacher, she even took one pupil on the train to Scarborough to sit her eleven plus examination. Frank Green, Jack's brother, who had a printing business in town, gave the young girl a lift home in his two-seater Morris convertible.

The large landowner, Mr Lotherington, once again approached Johnson Robinson to offer him Wragby Farm, which was three miles across the moor, just off the Scarborough to Whitby road. His sons John and Jim along with daughter Ann ran the farm and their father checked on them weekly.

Animals enjoying a drink at Church Farm pond

Jim Robinson at Burniston Show with first prize winner.

In 1934 driving tests became compulsory for all new drivers and the 30 mph speed limit was introduced in built up areas. Prospects in general were beginning to look brighter, with less unemployment and a reduction in income tax. Splashes of colour were introduced on illustrations in holiday brochures and general advertising. Raven Hall Hotel commenced the summer season with a new attraction: an open air sea water swimming bath. This pool measured one hundred by thirty-five feet and had light cream-coloured walls and base. The one-and-a-half-inch thick cement, referred to as 'Cullamix' was placed on to the reinforced concrete floor and then polished; the walls were treated in the same way. The surround of the pool was laid with four-foot square green slabs, and the depth of water ranged from three to six-foot. Water was pumped direct from the sea up the cliff through a filtration and chlorination plant. Once in place, the running of the pool was left in the capable hands of George Duck who was in charge of maintenance at the hotel. I was told that he knew every valve and pipe of the complex central heating system.

The hotel now had Mr Cooper at the helm along with a proficient secretary, who happened to be his sister-in-law, Miss Phyllis Donson. Much later, my memories of this woman are of a smart, raven-haired lady with dark-rimmed spectacles and ruby red lipstick. Also a new restaurant had been added where much of the cuisine of vegetables, tomatoes and eggs continued to be supplied by their own farm. The milk and cream was from the pedigree Jersey cows, which had all successfully passed the tuberculin test. The restaurant also doubled up as a ballroom where a small orchestra played for dancing two or three times a week. A few years later a glass screen surround was put in place at the pool and with additional seating, this proved to be a welcome refuge on breezy days. Two hard surface tennis courts were also added to these improvements. Until the mid-thirties visitors travelled by rail or car, but that was about change with the arrival of the 114 bus service from Scarborough, which used the hotel entrance as its terminus. As well as his normal duties, Mr Cooper also enjoyed his regular visits to the local Men's Club meetings in the Memorial Hall. One evening he invited members of the Robin Hood's Bay Institute to be his guests at Raven Hall and to compete in various games against the Ravenscar team.

Raven Hall brochure of 1935

*Above: Drawing of Swimming pool and tennis courts at Raven Hall.
Below: Freda, Dale and Edith Birdsall, at Raven Hall pool*

The Londesborough and Capitol cinemas were soon to be augmented by a third that would be vastly different with a modernistic Art Deco facade. The new Odeon cinema had Ravenscar connections insomuch that a substantial amount of bricks had been supplied for this new building by the village brickyard company. This was told to me at a very young age by my father John. The grand opening on May 28th 1936 featured the film 'The Ghost Goes West' starring Robert Donat, but the highlight of the evening was the personal appearance of Charles Laughton the Hollywood actor, who was born in Scarborough. However, Mr Carter's company, New Century Pictures was not pleased with this development stating, "This would be opposed on the grounds that the present accommodation in the town's cinemas was more than ample". These objections were to no avail.

The Odeon cinema as it is today, now known as the Stephen Joseph Theatre.

Billy Stubbs and Tom Duck at the brickworks

Five new bungalows had sprung up in the mid-thirties. Mr Thompson (Pal) retired from Springfield Farm and moved into his new abode near the village hall. He was remembered for having an angry bull, which on one occasion when the children were leaving school had escaped and charged down the road, snorting and swishing his tail from side to side. In an instant the youngsters scrambled to safety over the nearest wall. Mr and Mrs Brigham with their son Bruce acquired the first property to be built on the road from Staintondale approaching the windmill. Mr and Mrs Temple and family left the Coastguard Cottages leaving their friendly neighbours Mr and Mrs Brown (the local midwife) at the White Cottage and moved into 'Heathercroft'. Mr Temple, a roadman or linesman, could often be seen working alongside his counterpart Mr Taylor, and together they did an excellent job of keeping the gullies and gutters completely clear of all debris. Hence in those days, floods were never seen on the local roads. Mr and Mrs Bullas took up residence in another new property near Station House. Mrs Bullas was known as the 'Poppy Lady' doing her door to door annual collection for the British Legion. Probably the last bungalow to be completed, Pollard Cottage opposite the church, was funded by Mr Carter.

Above: The 'Coastguard Cottages'
Below: Mr & Mrs Brown outside the 'White Cottage'

Ravenscar properties and inhabitants had a lucky escape on Sunday April 18th 1937, when an R.A.F. fighter plane crashed after hitting a wall and an electricity pole on Church Road, cutting off the supply to the whole village. Dr. B.G. Forman from nearby Cloughton attended the injured pilot who was then taken to Scarborough Hospital. The Yorkshire Post reported: *'Villagers released an R.A.F. pilot who was hanging by his safety belt over the side of his wrecked plane after he had crashed in thick fog at Ravenscar...................*

Miss Smallwood, who works at Crag Hill Hotel, and Mrs Brand, who lives in the cottage which the plane missed, saw the crash. Mrs Brand's two children, Eileen, and John, were standing near the cottage and a large piece of the broken electricity pole fell within a yard of them.'

Newspaper cutting from the Yorkshire Post showing plane wreckage

George VI was crowned on May 12th at Westminster Abbey and grand celebrations were planned in the village replicating the coronation of the late King George V. Unfortunately, this time these festivities were overshadowed by atrocious weather. Events were transferred inside where possible, while in common with other villages in the area, sports were postponed to a later date or cancelled.

Our government was keeping a close eye on developments in Europe and the misery created by Hitler with the persecution of the Jewish community. By 1938, with even more unrest on the continent, Parliament decided to prepare for the inevitable. Air raid shelters were built in all the cities and early warning systems were set up in the South East. During late September of that year the first radar station in Yorkshire was assembled at Ravenscar beacon, before two were built at Danby and Staxton Wold. Three skilled RAF personnel arrived to erect the early warning station. Initially they had standard wireless poles and a telescopic tower, but early in 1939 these were replaced with two ninety-foot towers. At first these young men slept in a wooden hut on site and for washing facilities and at meal times they would go down to Mill Farm, the home of Mr and Mrs Jim Thompson. Eventually a perimeter wire was put in place with power laid on from School Lane. Comfortable lodgings soon became available with Mr and Mrs Jack Green at the newly-built Pollard Cottage. One of these servicemen, Frank Bostock Roberts, never dreamt that shortly after arriving in the village he would meet the love of his life. This young lady was Gladys, the daughter of Mr W.B. Cross who lived at Bell Hill Farm. Within a few months, Mr Roberts was posted to Egypt and it would be almost six years before the young couple were reunited.

In September war was declared after Germany invaded Poland.

Frank Roberts who was posted to Ravenscar

Bell Hill Farm

Later in the year many local men were conscripted into the forces, including two brothers, George and Stephen, sons of George Dale and Elsie Birdsall. George enlisted in the Merchant Navy whilst Stephen joined the Royal Air Force. With more distressing stories emerging from abroad, thoughts of what lay ahead were on everyone's mind.

The Birdsall family with George and Stephen in centre

Throughout the summer months, life carried on as normal. Cricket continued to increase in popularity, not only as a competitive sport, but as a vital form of relaxation. Along with the men, women were also keen to join. As there were not sufficient ladies interested to form a team in Ravenscar and Staintondale, those wishing to participate had to join the Cloughton and Burniston Ladies' Club. One young woman, Mary Consitt from Rigg Hall, Staintondale, practised with players from Ravenscar, whose captain, Johnson Robinson, would eventually become her father-in-law. All lady cricketers in the surrounding area bowled underarm, but Mary decided that if the men could bowl overarm, then so could she, which took the opposition by surprise. The next season more players followed suit, and it wasn't long before all ladies bowled over arm and were much more competitive by doing so. Mary attained fame locally as the very first lady overarm bowler! The team played in the Buckrose Ladies' League. Mary went into bat at number four and usually opened the bowling.

Mary Consitt, back row second from left

A new incumbent arrived at St Hilda's Ravenscar. The Rev. W.R. Spalding Wray succeeded Rev. N.H. Cox who had been vicar of the parish for the previous six years. Mrs Wray was responsible for establishing the local Girl Guide Association in the village. The Guides wore light blue and the Rangers' uniform was navy.

Girl Guides pictured in church yard, Ravenscar
Back row left to right: Maggie Ward, Ann Robinson, Unknown, Mrs Wray, Faith Temple, Doris Temple, Marjorie Thompson.
Front row left to right: Audrey Brand, Rita Steele, Freda Stubbs.

Following two decades of relative peace, the war effort started all over again by raising funds to purchase wool, which the women knitted into scarves, socks and mittens, for soldiers stationed both away and in the village. The troubles did not deter members of the Women's Institute from holding their annual Christmas whist drive and dance. The players enjoyed a light supper before dancing the night away until 2 am, always making the most of such events as if it was their last.

***

CHAPTER SEVEN

CASUALTIES AND HEROES

With fear of an imminent invasion; as Italy declared war on Britain, and Germany invaded France, two anti-aircraft searchlights were set up in the area. The first one was near Ashyard Farm, the home of Mr & Mrs Rayment, and the other was adjacent to the Nissen huts in Mr Johnson Robinson's field at Wragby. Four masts appeared at the 'Beacon Top'; two of the men working on this new R.A.F radar station were the Scarlett brothers from Scarborough. Another station, established in Mr and Mrs White's field at Bent Rigg Farm, situated between the railway line and coastguard outlook, it was guarded by the Northumberland Fusiliers. About the same time, a rotating aerial was placed on a circular concrete base with a brick surround in Johnson's beacon field. Grandfather would have been highly amused that in future years many people would assume it was a sheepfold.

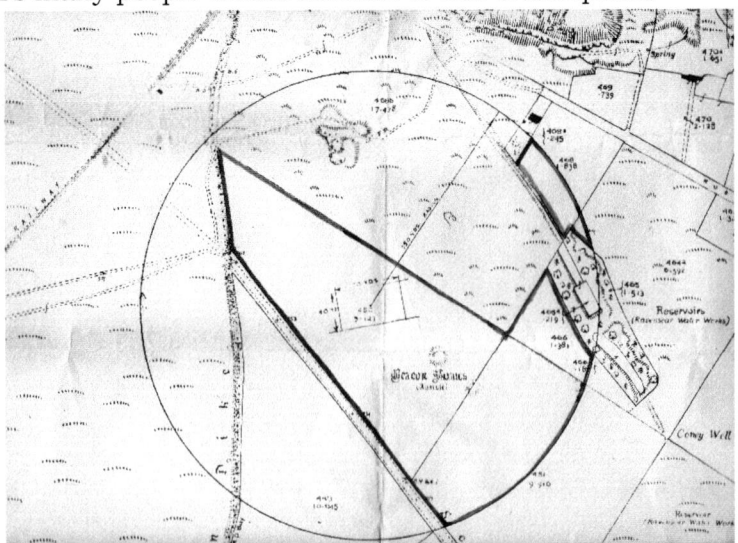

Map of the rotating aerial

The radar station buildings as they are today

As Germany advanced, our forces retreated to the coast and the dramatic rescue operation from Dunkirk began. A large armada of small boats including Scarborough's pleasure boats 'The Regal Lady' and 'Coronia' were sent to collect surviving soldiers stranded on the beaches.

Meanwhile, local men still at home working the land joined the Home Guard. Amongst them were Harry Robinson and Ted Duck. Firemen Arthur and George Cross, along with their father Mr W. B. Cross, the local Air Raid Precautions Warden, also played a vital role. As in the First World War, Johnson Robinson was appointed Special Constable.

The Women's Voluntary Service was put in charge of the many evacuees, including children and two teachers from Hull.

Harry Robinson and Ted Duck in the Home Guard

Olivia Street recalls a brief stay at Bell Hill Farm, before she was billeted with Mrs Leonard at 'Mountain Ash' Staintondale.

Mr W.B.Cross – Air Raid Warden

One August morning, John, still in shock, mounted the pony and galloped across the moor to Church Farm bearing upsetting news. In the early hours an enemy bomber had made an unsuccessful attempt to take out the searchlight, but sadly eight cows had been killed. One poor thing, a red poll, still alive with a severed foot, was shot to avoid further suffering. The bull ran to a hawthorn hedge for cover, but the aircraft flew round again to complete the massacre and peppered him with bullets; needless to say he bled to death.

There was a notable change of atmosphere with the absence of visitors strolling along the Marine Esplanade enjoying the unspoilt beauty of the coast. Three shelters built for the town that never materialised were virtually deserted. Raven Hall, which had been a success story as a prime hotel, was requisitioned by the Army preparing for combat, and the owners Mr and Mrs Cooper moved into Scarborough. Mr and Mrs Wrightson who had run the boarding house in Station Square had recently left to live near Pickering. The camping coaches on the railway siding were also casualties of this terrible war.

The Women's Institute, in addition to singing 'Jerusalem' at the beginning of each monthly meeting, now observed a one minute silence to pray for anyone in danger from the enemy onslaught. Local dances and other fundraising events were held in aid of the Spitfire Fund and Nursing Association. The brickworks shut down and workers were either laid off or joined up to fight for their country. There were two possible reasons for the closure, the lack of demand for bricks or maybe the glow from the kiln was considered a high security risk. From then on the disused yard became a permanent winter abode for 'Laughing Jack'. Previously this man of the road had sheltered in the hay loft at Church Farm, but before he was allowed into the barn his matches were confiscated to avoid any accidents.

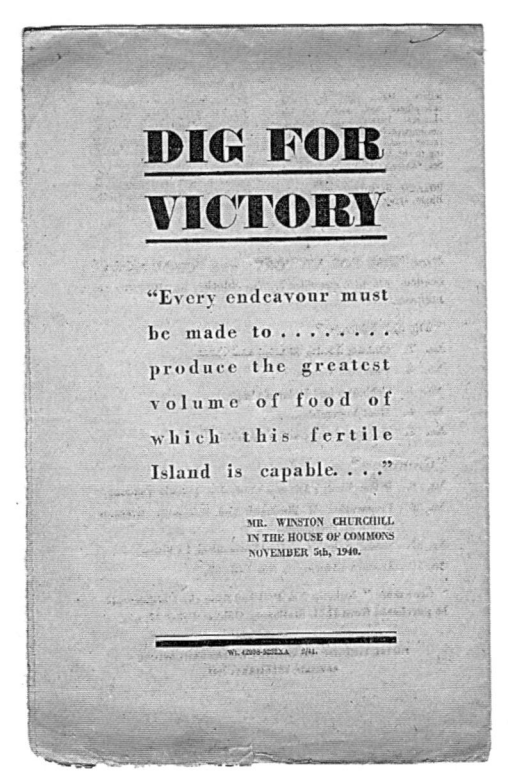

Dig for Victory pamphlet

Rationing on several commodities had already been put in place when Prime Minister Winston Churchill announced that all garden and allotment owners should 'Dig for Victory'. Consequently, the Ministry of Agriculture and Fisheries published a leaflet that was delivered to all householders. This outlined *"how to crop your ground to the best advantage, so as to get vegetables all the year round, please study it carefully and carry out the advice it contains".* In line with this, farmers were ploughing their grass fields and sowing corn to increase the grain production and planting huge amounts of potatoes and turnips. However, a crop of wheat was partly decimated when two tanks of the many stationed in the village drove across a cornfield taking a short cut from Raven Hall to Station Square. This seemed to be a very irresponsible thing to do when every grain of corn was precious, but apparently they would have been under orders to do so.

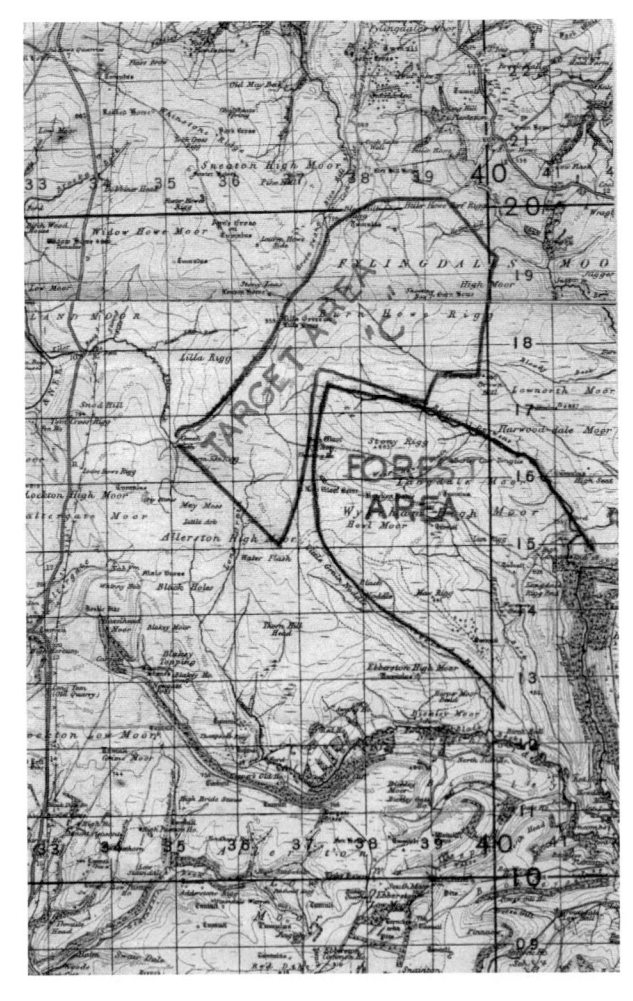

Target Area for the three large guns

There were large numbers of young soldiers practising various manoeuvres as part of the Allied preparations for their ultimate goal, the invasion against German-occupied France. In France the roads would no doubt be heavily mined and the alternative route would be across fields and through hedges. Bofors guns, double-barrelled, automatic anti-aircraft weapons, were strategically lined along a wall near the mill firing at targets trailed by low-flying aircraft. One onlooker claimed the exercise was aborted early as gunfire was so erratic that the planes took off in the opposite direction! Also regularly, three large guns were positioned at a high altitude. The sites used were the Beacon at Ravenscar, Reasty Bank at Harwood Dale and Blue Bank near Sleights. Local artillery practice days were arranged and a target area designated. Units would be allowed to shoot into this area up to six days each month. Farmers, including John and Jim at Wragby, were notified that all stock and persons must be one mile outside the area. Jim commented that in order to comply with those instructions all the animals and themselves had to be on the coastal side of the farmhouse.

A previous benefactor of the village, Mr Sydney Carter passed away at his home in Scarborough. Locals remembered him for his extreme generosity especially to the church, and also the immense pleasure that he had given to them as children with his advice and guidance when staging theatrical productions in the village hall.

Several residents had been on the move at this time. Mr Goodall replaced Mr Leake as stationmaster, which left the post of church organist vacant, but the very capable Ernest Thompson accepted the position and was aided by Billy Stubbs pumping the organ.

Ernest Thompson

Mr Fairhurst took over the chicken farm by the old golf links from Mr Pyne. The derelict golf pavilion opened by the Earl of Cranbrooke in the previous century had totally disappeared. Mr Blakeley had died leaving Cliff House empty. Jack and Harriet Green moved from Pollard Cottage to Coney Springs, which had been built for Mr and Mrs Pickering, who moved into the detached house a few hundred yards away at Broom Rise. The gardens were artistically landscaped and featured a meandering footpath leading down to Crag Lane. In several places climbing roses adorned trellised archways. Mr Salathiel Gibson with his wife and daughter followed Mrs Newsome at Gorse Cottage, and the Ripley family had taken over Springfield Farm.

In contrast, Loring Road residents were very settled and content to live in their properties between thirty and fifty-plus years. Number one was occupied by the Brewers; Connie was a member of both Ravenscar and Staintondale Women's Institutes. She attended the Staintondale Methodist Chapel and played the hymns for Sunday School. Next door were Mr and Mrs Shippey. Several years later I can remember Mrs Shippey in a long skirt and apron, wearing plimsolls. At number three Mr Goforth lived with his sister. He regularly attended the Men's Club and was umpire for the Cricket Club. Previously they had been at the mill for several years. The Jackson family lived at number four, and had moved up from Ewefield Farm on Browside. Several daughters went into the nursing profession, some of whom became matrons. Mr Jackson sporting an open-necked shirt, whatever the weather, made a daily trek across the moor to the ganister works until he was seventy two years old.

A large piece of agricultural land along the cliff top, which stretched from Hammond Road southwards beyond Station Square, became available to rent at one pound an acre per year. Johnson Robinson took advantage of this offer.

In September 1941, tragic news hit the parish with the death of Chief Officer George Dale Bolton Birdsall, a master mariner with the Merchant Navy who had been killed in action. One lady said to me recently "he was a lovely polite lad".

Loring Road houses as they are today. Inset pictures of residents who lived there in the 40s

Miss Brewer   Mr Shippey   Mr Goforth   Mr & Mrs Jackson

A yearly report of the Cloughton District Nursing Association showed that through entertainment, Ravenscar had subscribed three pounds. The association covered eleven other villages in addition to Ravenscar and Staintondale. Representatives on the committee for Ravenscar were Mrs Robinson and Mrs Thompson; Mrs Cross, Mrs Drake, and F.L.P. Sturge represented Staintondale. The village managed to get together their own quintet when arranging dances for the fund and this helped to boost the profit for the evening.

Those making up the band were George Cross, Arthur Cross, Mrs Ousley, Mrs Goodall and Miss Brewer.

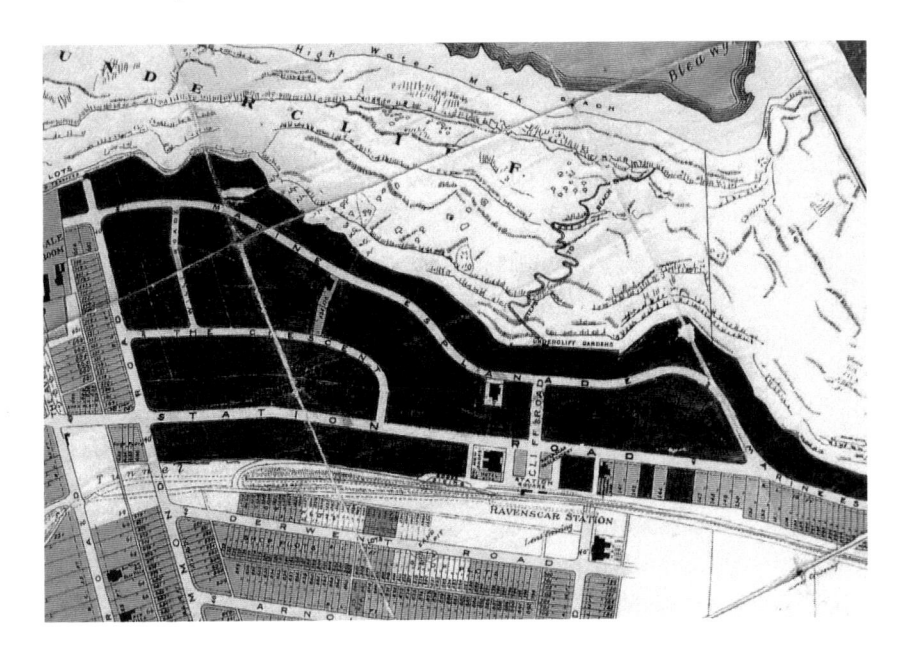

Land rented from the Estate Company

In February of 1944, it was announced that the Air Force had successfully carried out a major bombing campaign of Berlin. Although a dangerous mission, out of almost one thousand aircraft (figures vary in different reports), comparatively few failed to return. However, in Ravenscar everyone's thoughts were with the seven men who lost their lives as a Halifax bomber crashed near Stoupe Brow. It had been attempting to make an emergency landing on the moor when everything went disastrously wrong in the last few minutes. The plane rolled down a steep escarpment on the edge of the moor leaving a trail of devastation and the wreckage was scattered over a wide area of farmland next to the railway line. A farmer from Ladysmith Farm went to the scene the following day and after seeing the carnage told his wife not to go anywhere near until the debris was cleared.

Although these were terrible times, local villages tried to make life as normal as possible by arranging various events throughout the war.

Chief Officer George Dale Bolton Birdsall

An agricultural show had been organised at Staintondale in 1942 and many residents of Ravenscar entered their produce in the various classes. This was chiefly a horticultural show. The following year, obviously very pleased with the support for the previous one, it was decided to make this an annual event. An even bigger success followed with two hundred and seventy entries in both agricultural and horticultural classes. *'Nearly four hundred people paid for admission to the school, where the exhibits were displayed. Tea was served in the Village Hall and was followed by a dance'.* The show went from strength to strength with entries increasing annually.

Yet another tragedy in the parish was when Mr and Mrs Birdsall's second son Stephen also died for his country. Warrant Officer Stephen Dale Birdsall who had served with the Royal Air Force was only twenty four years old. A memorial plaque to these two brave young men can be seen in Ravenscar Church. I remember at about the age of ten, gazing round the church in boredom when the vicar was delivering his sermon and feeling such sorrow when I realised the two names listed were from the same family.

Warrant Officer Stephen Dale Birdsall

As the threat of an invasion diminished and the liberation of Europe began it was obvious that the war was drawing to a close.

On November 1st 1944 it was decided to 'stand down' the Home Guard. Members from Ravenscar and Staintondale had to hand in all arms and ammunition to the Platoon headquarters at Staintondale Village Hall. They were allowed to keep their badges and all items of clothing, which included the 'greatcoat' and boots that would be very useful for years to come. The final parade of the 10th North Riding Battalion took place on Sunday December 3rd at Scarborough Cricket Ground. They wore their uniforms with pride for the last time as they marched through the town to Falsgrave and turned into St. John's Road where they were finally dismissed.

Young Allan Green keeping guard on a haycock!

Three children were feeling peckish after school and one boy with a penknife at the ready, climbed over a wall into a field of turnips. He pulled a turnip from the ground, and after topping and tailing it, but before coming back into view, put the feast under his cap. Down the road, the trio entered the churchyard and once out of sight the raw turnip was shared out and devoured in a matter of minutes. Another source of amusement was collecting used tracer bullets; the youngsters competed with each other to find the winner.

A discarded box containing Molotov cocktails was found hidden behind a stone wall. In the wrong hands these fire bombs could be very dangerous, but a local man used them for several years to light the annual bonfire on November 5th in Station Square.

There was great news and relief when Mr Frank Roberts returned safely. The young couple were reunited and after such a long time apart enjoyed a very happy wedding day. They eventually moved into 'Ranworth', adjacent to the church, where Frank Wrightson had lived for some years.

Ravenscar House ceased to be a boarding house and became three separate dwellings. Miss Cleasby, a retired headmistress and her many cats had moved into number one. By 1945 Mr and Mrs Alan Johnson were living at number two. He was a builder by trade but also had the job of reading the water meters and collecting water rates at various properties belonging to the Estate Company. At number three Mr McCabe the station porter and his wife managed the post office, which had been transferred from the Thompson family next door who continued to have the general stores at number four.

The day arrived that the whole nation had been waiting for. Peace had come at last when VE day was celebrated on the 8th May 1945. In Ravenscar as in other villages, they arranged a party. Bunting, which had been used for the Coronation bedecked the village hall and all residents were invited to bring whatever food they could spare, including potted meat sandwiches, jellies, cakes and buns. A band of local musicians played for dancing in the evening.

Mr and Mrs Morris had left Crag Hill and the new occupier was Mrs Norman and her daughter Evelyn who worked as a nurse at Scarborough Hospital. Mr Norman had connections with the tea industry and lived in India before returning to Ravenscar where he died.

The Rev. Arthur Garbutt became the Vicar of Ravenscar, Staintondale, and Howdale in the spring of 1946; he and his wife soon formed a long lasting friendship with my grandparents. Prior to this he had been out of the country for almost five years with the British Army in North Africa and Italy as padre to a Durham Light Infantry Brigade. After settling in the village, like many others, he decided it would be helpful to have his own supply of free range eggs and bought some 'point of lay pullets'. I'm sure life at the vicarage would be a safe sanctuary from the cooking pot as 'old boilers'. One day, seeing Grandfather and Harry in a nearby field thinning turnips, he asked to join them; at first this was refused but after much persuasion Johnson gave in. The vicar no doubt found working on the land therapeutic and a refreshing pastime away from his normal duties. He joined the Men's Club and occasionally played cricket with the local team. The austere interior of the vicarage needed a facelift to create, if possible, a more homely atmosphere, quite a mammoth task. Three men arrived from Rowntrees of Scarborough, a famous department store in Westborough, and lived with the family until the work was completed at a total cost of £194.14s 8d. Mrs Garbutt ran the Mothers' Union, which possibly started about the same time as the one at Staintondale Church. Later that year she was elected to the Women's Institute committee. Mrs Pope, who had recently moved to 'Sunnyside', next door to the village hall, took on the role of secretary. Two new members, Mrs G. Cross and Mrs McCabe who had recently moved into the village, were welcomed at the Christmas meeting.

The railway played its part in despatches. Several years earlier both Mr & Mrs Jackson who ran the old post office wished their final resting place to be at Lythe near Whitby from whence they came. On both occasions their pitch pine coffins, made by Mr Leonard the joiner of Staintondale, were transported by rail to nearby Sandsend. Also, during the forties a resident wished to be cremated, although in those days the nearest crematorium was at Lawnswood just outside Leeds. When the day arrived they all set off by train, the family, the coffin, the funeral director and the vicar! Upon the return journey they missed their connection from Scarborough to Ravenscar resulting in a two-hour wait for the next train. One of the mourners suddenly noticed that the Odeon cinema across the road from the station was showing a western film which was about to start, so he approached the vicar for his opinion whether it was suitable for a funeral party to attend. The family were much relieved with the reply "I think it is an excellent idea, much better than shivering on the platform".

The Coastguard practices hadn't changed much in recent years and the life-saving equipment was still kept on a cart in the Coastguard Hut ready to be yoked to the horse 'Banker', harnessed by Harry Robinson. There were a number of practices a year, when a rocket attached to a rope was tied to the hawser and then fired along the undercliff. The village boys had to retrieve the rocket as it was refuelled and used again. Ravenscar was part of the Yorkshire and Lincolnshire Division but under the command of Whitby. However, in January 1947 they were issued with new instructions that superseded all other orders that had been used for the 'Heath Jackstay Drill'. With this reorganisation, auxiliaries of the Ravenscar Life Saving Apparatus Company were each given a permanent number from one to twelve.
1. E. Thompson, 2. R. Rayment, 3. R. Rennison,
4. J. Robinson,   5. A. Garbutt, 6. T. Lightfoot, 7. T. France,
8. S. Steele, 9. H. Robinson, 10. W. France, 11. T. White,
12. G. Duck.
Listed are three examples from the complicated instructions:

'1 and 10. Rocket machine. Place in the most convenient position.
4 and 8.   Whip box. Placed 8 paces to leeward of rocket line box. Whip box placed in rear of line box.
7 and 9.   Triangle. Placed lee side of whip box. Number 7 will then provide flag or lamp and attend to signals. Number 9 will hand gear from cart or lorry before providing triangle.'

The winter of 1947 brought with it a few surprises. Wray's bread van doing its weekly deliveries during the first week of February succumbed to the blizzard conditions which quickly formed drifts. It was abandoned at Raven Hall and remained there for about six weeks. Much to the delight of the youngsters the school bus did not make the journey, likewise the United Bus had to end its journey five miles away at Cloughton. Three weeks later there was still no sign of any road transport coming through, and even the snow plough seemed ineffective. Until now the mail had been coming by train and the milk had been transported to the Whitby Co-op dairy. Now the never-ending winter also caused chaos on the railways and blocked the line between Fylingthorpe and Staintondale. At Wragby Farm the milk churns were taken by horse and sledge to Fylingthorpe station, travelling cross country over walls and hedges hidden by several feet of frozen snow. The young men in Ravenscar pulled their toboggans to Staintondale station to collect provisions for the village. A friend of the family recollected....

'the snow brought everything to a standstill for almost two months, it was the longest School Holiday I ever had, and there were no trains so the School Mistress was unable to get from Scarborough. To help clear the roads a team of Italian Prisoners of War somehow got through to Ravenscar and were accommodated at the Village Hall. They started to dig the road out at the Raven Hall Hotel and got as far as the Windmill and the road would be snowed in again, there was another team working their way up from Cloughton. Most people of Ravenscar were well prepared for this harsh weather, with candles, paraffin, coal and food and had the wherewithal to make bread. Even in good weather we had electricity power cuts, many houses did not have electricity; they had the lovely soft light given out by paraffin pressure lamps. To power their wirelesses they had accumulators, people used to bring them to Jack Green to be recharged about once a week, usually on a Saturday. They would have two, one with Jack Green recharging and the other one at home powering the radio'.

After this severe winter, which would be talked about for decades, the country was blessed with a glorious summer.

Above: Ravenscar in the grip of winter

Below: Clearing the main road into the village

What a relief to the general store and post office including the residents, when the delivery of food and provisions returned to normal. Mr Sedman from Burniston was still delivering meat weekly, but others in the village preferred to use a Robin Hood's Bay butcher for their Sunday joints. One day at Station Square a joint of meat went missing from a householder's pantry and a bloody trail led to the back door. 'Bill', Jack Green's dog was blamed, he was known as a scrounger and roamer. He once took up residence at the Raven Hall and a short while after decided to be more adventurous and set up home at the Victoria Hotel in Robin Hood's Bay. He was a loveable streetwise old boy and Jack had bought him from Mr Hufton with whom he shared coastguard duties. Milk was delivered by Geoff White with his hand cart from Bent Rigg Farm; Church Road Farm and Church Farm were also suppliers. Mr Brand collected coal and coke from the station goods siding and distributed them to the residents by horse and cart. When the weather had improved Mr Shippey was able to supply fish again. The stationmaster, station porter and the vicar enjoyed catching their own fish. They scrambled down the cliff path below Station Square, which was quite a difficult descent, and on the second part there was a rope to help.

The tourist industry came alive with the re-opening of Raven Hall Hotel on May 22nd for the 1947 summer season. It must have taken Mr Cooper several months to refurbish the premises after the military had departed leaving the beautiful floors scuffed by heavy army boots. Visitors were asked to bring their own towels and soap, but if staying five days or more guests had to take their ration books. A ten per cent service charge was added to all accounts. Unfortunately the roughly finished Marine Esplanade had been further rutted by the tanks travelling back and forth. However, two of the shelters and the steps down to the rocks were still intact for the holidaymakers to enjoy.

The money from the bazaar this year was earmarked for the installation of electricity at the church. Mr Steele's four-piece band from Ruston provided music for the dance (he was the brother of Sid Steele the head gardener at Raven Hall

Hotel). Once sufficient funds were raised it would no longer be necessary to carry urns of boiling water across from Church Farm when the church rooms were in use for Mothers' Union meetings and other socials.

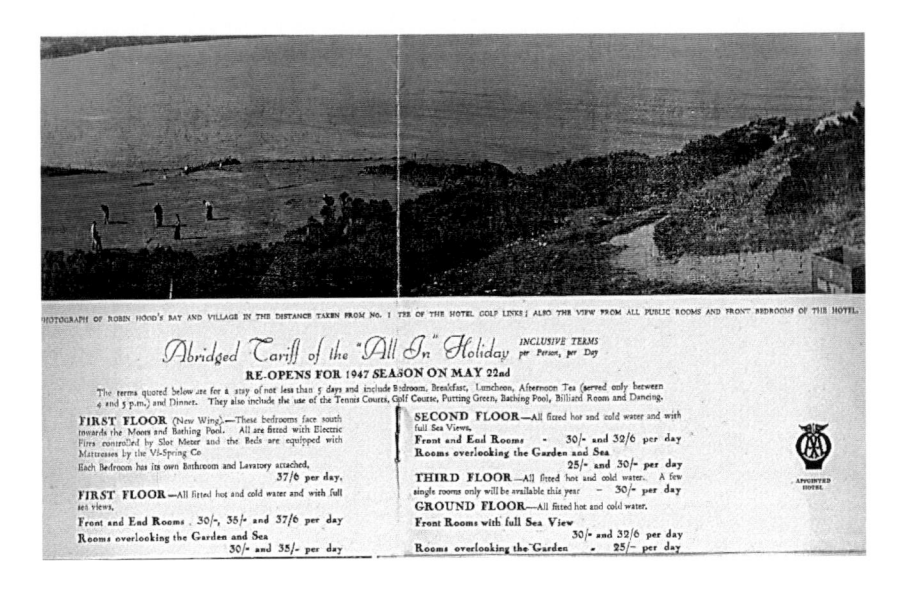

Picture taken from Raven Hall Hotel's 1947 brochure

At the end of the cricket season the club held a whist drive and dance in the village hall. Mr J.R. Cooper, the club president and owner of the cricket field, congratulated the members on a successful season both in league and friendly matches under the captaincy of Mr Sid Steele, his first year leading the team. Friendly games were often played on Sunday afternoons between the home side and a team of visitors staying at the hotel. At the end of his speech the president presented Johnson Robinson with a chiming clock and all present sang 'For he's a jolly good fellow'. The clock bears the inscription: -

'Presented to Mr J Robinson captain of Ravenscar Cricket Club for the past 30 years, by fellow members past and present in appreciation of his long association with the Club. 1947.'

Mr Cooper gave a bat to the club's up and coming young player who had showed consistent progress in the game. This was presented to John Lightfoot.

The retiring captain, Johnson Robinson

A motorbike was the most popular form of transport in the village due to it being a cost-effective mode of getting around. Jack Green, Walter France and Vincent Ripley were amongst the many bikers. The Reverend Garbutt had also discarded his bicycle for a Velocette motorbike and his son Michael along with Allan Green had jumped at the chance to have a go at playing on Mr Ripley's motorcycle.

The next generation of the Robinson family were preparing to leave their remote farm near the Flask Inn just three miles west of Ravenscar, for Church Farm which was to be their new home. Myself as a young girl and my brother were not looking forward to leaving our birthplace, which had been such a secure environment.

Allan Green and Michael Garbutt revving up Vincent Ripley's motorbike

The new family Robinson: John, Eileen. Alan and Mary, and below, Eileen's first love

CHAPTER EIGHT

'THE STORY OF MY LIFE'

With the promise of happier times ahead, Ravenscar provided a safe environment for a young girl to live in. Grandfather Robinson retired to Cloughton after working the farm for nearly forty years and seeing his large family benefit from all his endeavours. We had left our friendly neighbours Mr and Mrs Place at the Flask Cafe, and moved into Church Farm next door to Pollard Cafe. The occupants Mr and Mrs Herefield served appetising light lunches and high teas, on the menu were ham and eggs, poached eggs and beans on toast. I craved for a piece of yummy cake or a bowl of fruit and jelly as I waited patiently for my ice cream wafer. After placing one biscuit in the base of a metal mould it was then carefully packed with ice cream and topped by a second biscuit. Finally, when the completed ice cream wafer was handed over on a piece of greaseproof paper, every lick was savoured.

Ice cream treats

Two new bungalows had recently been built, one on the left approaching the windmill where Mr and Mrs Nelson lived with their son and daughter. The second was just before the school in which Mrs Bedford resided. This was built on plots numbered 237 and 238 originally purchased by Mr Place.

The first television aerial in Ravenscar was seen strapped to the chimney breast at Coney Springs. Jack Green had become the proud owner of a Bush nine-inch screen model in a brown Bakelite case. It was purchased from Goods in Scarborough, just in time for the F.A. Cup Final which many locals came to watch, including Jack's father-in-law George Lightfoot. Jack later acquired a magnifier which boosted the picture size.

The Reverend Garbutt's final visit to the Men's Club

Back row: left to right, R. Rennison, L. Place, F. Roberts, T. France, W. Stubbs, H. Robinson, R. Brooks.

Middle row: J. Vale, S. Steele, F. Farrer, J. Cooper, A. Cross, G. Gibson, J. Green, W. France, G. Cross, G. Duck.

Front row: J.R. Cooper, W.B. Cross, T. Lightfoot, W. Goforth, Rev.A. Garbutt, J. Robinson, T. White, E. Thompson, J. Fox.

Sitting on the floor: E. Brand, G. White, J. Lightfoot, M. France.

The Rev. Arthur Garbutt

Men's Club social

The very popular Reverend Garbutt and his family had moved to Brafferton. The new incumbent would have to be a very special person to fill the gap of his predecessor. In fact, the new vicar and his wife filled two vacancies. Rev. J. Stoddart Sellers' wife, a schoolteacher, succeeded Miss Suggitt who had travelled daily from Scarborough by train. There were about twelve children at the school aged between five and eleven. Older children went on the school bus to Scalby County Modern and those who attended the Boys' High, Girls' High, or Graham Sea Training schools in Scarborough caught the service bus. My brother and I were pupils at Fylingdales Church of England School. We journeyed by rail along the picturesque route to Robin Hood's Bay, a view we did not appreciate at the time. The one thing I dreaded after alighting from the train was walking over the crossing, sometimes only a yard in front of the huge imposing engine. On the return trip I was delighted to see daylight at the end of the tunnel; sometimes the synonymous pleasant smell oozing from a steam locomotive could be overpowering as we passed through the tunnel, especially if the carriage windows weren't shut! In bad weather it was quite exciting when the train got into difficulties attempting the incline from the brickworks. One fine day, rather than waiting an hour at the station, we decided to walk home from school. This trek took us through delightful countryside across farm fields into woodland, over a footbridge straddling the small beck and into a grass field, then a steep climb took us to the railway crossing at Ladysmith Farm in Howdale. Nearing our destination we came along the track above the brickyard, which was a welcoming sight as the final lap of our marathon was but a few hundred yards away.

As in other villages, a dentist visited the school with his mini surgery complete with gas bottle, all set up inside a caravan. One boy was told that he needed several teeth extracting but his mother decided to use a Scarborough dentist, which was a big mistake as the poor lad had a painful experience resulting in cocaine poisoning.

We attended Sunday School every week. In the mornings Mr Roberts took his Triumph Mayflower full of children to the

Methodist Chapel where Mrs Ward was our teacher assisted by Miss Brewer who also accompanied the singing on the harmonium. My favourite was 'Jesus wants me for a sunbeam'. After enjoying our roast beef and Yorkshire puddings it was time to get ready for afternoon Sunday School in St. Hilda's church room. This was run by Miss Grace Thompson but was not as well supported as the morning service in the chapel. As if that wasn't enough we were expected to attend the fortnightly six o' clock Evensong with Ernest Thompson at the organ and David Steele pumping the bellows.

Double headed excursion train passing the brickyard

Going back to the Mayflower; it was an exciting experience to take a trip down on to the pebbled beach at Stoupe Beck. The car was over-laden with noisy youngsters including myself, keen to explore the rock pools and run about in the sand and seaweed. When playtime was over, every sand-covered child clambered aboard and with the car revved up, it gradually made the climb back up from the shore.

Autumn was a time for us to earn a few pennies by collecting rose hips, there were some beauties on the cliff top. We were paid around threepence a pound and this was organised nationally through the village schools. The end product, rosehip syrup was a good source of vitamin C. Boys in their late teens had also discovered a way of making extra cash. Until recently, the owners of the brickyard had been sending an employee to grease the machinery, but the local lads had also taken an interest in the mechanism housed within the buildings, they removed many ball bearings and other small items, which were sold to a scrap metal merchant. This obsolete blot on a beautiful landscape had become a dangerous place for young teenagers enjoying 'hide and seek' in the dilapidated kiln. One day their adventures went a little too far and proved just how unsafe this site could be. Three of them, (who shall remain nameless), feeling the cold, decided to climb into a disused water tank. After lighting a small fire, the obvious happened, and with smoke and flames being drawn to the entrance, they had to make a dash to safety. The following day one of the young lads came to the farm, with curly, singed eyebrows and hair. He admitted how foolish they had been.

A sight to behold, which is never seen nowadays, was the herring fleet, with flickering lights far out to sea, like the 'Milky Way' as they followed the shoals of herring southwards. In the event of stormy weather the fishing boats took shelter in the bay and that really was a spectacular scene not to be missed.

When the fifth of November came round, gorse bushes made the perfect base for a bonfire. Two of these gatherings come to mind for different reasons. The first occasion was when a member of staff from the Raven Hall brought a tractor and trailer stacked high with old blinds that had been used for the blackout during the war. I believe they also had sufficient to boost Goodall's fire at Springfield Farm. The other memorable time was 1956 when we had six inches of snow on the ground. Undaunted, the bonfire went ahead as usual. Having thrown the guy into the flames, we stood back and watched the firework display. The precious solitary rocket was balanced in the neck of a lemonade bottle, the Catherine wheel was pinned to the end of a hayfork, others including the Roman candle, volcano, shimmering cascade, chrysanthemum fountain and snow storm were lined up on a wooden plank supported by two posts. There were also a few bangers, crackers and aeroplanes not forgetting the hand held sparklers. We were more than satisfied with our night's entertainment, but today I know it could be classed as boring!

As Christmas drew near, grown-ups practised short sketches and plays for the annual concert held on the second Saturday in December. Miss Clapham and Miss Roberts who lived in part of the old Coastguard Cottages, taught at Fylinghall private school. These two ladies sat in on rehearsals and were very helpful with the costumes and dialogue. The end result was quite a polished affair. Connie Brewer and Harry Robinson were a popular double act performing in the sketches. Geoffrey White always sang a solo 'Yeoman of the Guard' or 'Keep Right on to the End of the Road' immediately spring to mind. Peter Nuttley, a permanent member of staff at the hotel who in his younger days had been a professional dancer, tutored the young ones. I remember him choreographing 'The Sailors Hornpipe' and 'Where Will the Baby's Dimple Be'. The village hall was always bursting at the seams for this event with many standing at the back.

In the week leading up to Christmas two groups of 'carollers' always came round; the Methodists from Staintondale and the Church of England from Ravenscar. By the time I was old enough to join them there were only two houses where the singers were invited indoors to partake of a much appreciated cup of tea and mince pie. These hospitable folk were Mr and Mrs Chitterden of Cliff House and Mrs Griffin from the bungalow near Station House. Christmas Eve arrived and our household followed the same festive customs every year. In the afternoon, the decorations which had been in use for years were brought out including old cardboard shapes that opened into attractive crepe paper bells. Mother hung streamers randomly across the living room ceiling, along with new homemade chains which we had assembled from coloured strips of paper. Each end was fastened by drawing pins to the old beams and after years of creating new pin holes, one would think there was an infestation of woodworm. The tree was never decorated until the evening and this job was allocated to my father. Again these trimmings were showing their age, and some very decorative birds had lost their feathered tails, and the spring clips holding them in place were spotted with rust. Holly and mistletoe were not allowed inside the house until Christmas morning. According to an old superstitious belief, to display it any earlier was considered unlucky. After breakfast the boys went 'Christmas shouting', usually to the farms in the village. They knocked on the door and then recited "We wish you a merry Christmas and a happy New Year, good luck to you and all you have, all through the year". Their reward would be a threepenny bit or a sixpence and if lucky, a mince pie and a very small glass of homemade bramble wine! The girls followed the same procedure on New Year's Day with a shortened version omitting "We wish you a merry Christmas". In some cases if they happened to be the first visitor of the day, an absolute must was to carry a piece of coal over the threshold. This was expected of the 'first footer', a tradition spanning years, bringing good luck to the household.

I remember the death of King George VI in 1952. The headmaster Mr Williams came into the classroom and whispered to our teacher Miss Church. She immediately burst into tears, which at the time I found very puzzling. After dabbing her eyes with a handkerchief and visibly upset she announced that the King was dead. The following year saw the community making plans to celebrate the coronation of Queen Elizabeth II. However due to the inclement weather some sports and the Maypole dancing had to be transferred from the grass tennis courts into the village hall. The highlight of the day was receiving our commemorative coronation mugs.

Newcomers Mr and Mrs Fox lived at 'Hillcrest' bungalow on Church Road which we passed on our way home from the station. It wasn't long before we were invited in to watch 'Andy Pandy' on television, a new experience for us. Within minutes Mrs Fox appeared with two mugs of Ovaltine. I couldn't stand the smell or the sickly taste so not daring to leave a drop, I gulped mine down quickly. Eventually enough was enough, and rather than refuse their kindness, we took an alternative route home, just to avoid the dreaded ordeal.

In the early hours of January 31st 1953 a terrific storm hit the east coast of Yorkshire. The Raven Hall pump house which supplied sea water to the swimming pool from the foot of the cliff, suffered irreparable damage, consequently from then on the pool had to use fresh water. The remains of the last cliff top shelter also succumbed to the brute force of the high winds and was totally destroyed. The severity of the wind was so great that wagon ropes had to be thrown over the chicken house and metal weights attached to the ends to prevent the roof from parting company with the shed. Another unusual sight in the village when gales of that magnitude were blowing in from the sea, was a brown sandy coloured foam akin to soapsuds that formed shapes bouncing like footballs up Raven Hall Road towards the church. On one occasion it reached the reservoir half a mile from the cliff top, and stretched for nearly one hundred yards.

The last shelter

After the death of Mr Lotherington, the farms and land he had owned for many years, passed to his daughter, Violet Mary Heppard from Scarborough. In 1953 she died and the tenants were given the opportunity to purchase their farms, the average price for each was seventeen hundred pounds. Miss White, a retired headmistress and sister of Mr Tom White, acquired the Lotherington holiday home 'Heather Cottage'. She took on the role of Sunday School teacher at St Hilda's and was also very supportive to children taking their eleven plus examination, giving them free weekly mathematics and English lessons.

With pupil numbers at the school dwindling each year, the closure of this amenity, which had opened in 1888, was inevitable. From Whitsuntide 1953, children were ferried three miles to Staintondale in a Trojan diesel mini coach where their new teacher, Miss Scales welcomed them.

It was a great relief when all rationing put in place during the Second World War finally came to an end, perhaps as well, because rabbit was now off the menu due to a countrywide outbreak of myxomatosis.

One day in poor visibility, a pilot decided to land his bi-plane before nightfall, he abandoned it behind a haystack. Without a word to anyone the stranger boarded the last train to Scarborough. The following morning he re-appeared, jumped into the cockpit, taxied to the top of the field, turned round, and took off. The police came round in the afternoon asking questions, but had to leave without any answers.

Ploughing days were still arranged as they had been for decades to help any new farmer arriving in the community. One noticeable difference, however was that horses had been replaced by tractors; the popular small grey Ferguson was a favourite. One farmer, unfamiliar with his new 'Fergie', lowered a plough using the hydraulic lever and unfortunately was unaware that it had sunk far too deep into the heavy clay soil. Try as he would, it remained firmly lodged in the ground as the front of the tractor threatened to rise. Totally embarrassed, he went to seek help from a farm labourer and it was eventually dug out manually. Prior to 1950 the only two farms possessing a tractor were Bell Hill and Bent Rigg, both with a Fordson tractor known for their metal spade-lug wheels.

Ploughing day at Mill Farm
Left to right: J.Wilson, R. Boddy, E. Pennock, J. Carr, H. Robinson

Above: Cows lining up for milking time
Below: Happy cats having a drink

Our Shire horse 'Metal' was semi-retired and only used for 'scruffling turnips' and 'banking up' potatoes. One of her final duties was to pull the straw covered wagon carrying Mr Salathiel Gibson's coffin from Gorse Cottage. This was a special request.

As times progressed the house at Church Farm remained as it had been at the turn of the century with a kitchen range, copper and outside toilet. In 1952 a telephone was connected to Robin Hood's Bay exchange, but other properties apart from those on School Lane were on the Cloughton line. The only other update was the installation of electricity in 1954.

Haymaking in Station Square

Cliff House, which had seen many different occupiers since the end of the war, was sold to the Catholic Church and used as a holiday home for the nuns. For some years Mr & Mrs Rymer from York had a caravan alongside the house, but with the change of ownership it was moved to the village hall. Very soon another caravan appeared which became the summer residence of the priest. Any Catholics who worked at Raven Hall were now able to take Mass in the house, saving them the journey into Scarborough.

'Gorse Cottage' - Copyright The Francis Frith Collection'

The camping coaches returned to the railway sidings, giving an alternative choice of self-catering breaks to holidaymakers. With a regular train service on the doorstep and situated a few hundred yards from the local shops, this made the ideal place for a relaxing holiday. Twice a week fresh crusty cobs and sliced 'Mother's Pride' loaves wrapped in red and white waxed paper were delivered to the Post Office managed by Mr and Mrs Crowcroft. All other provisions were available next door from Mr and Mrs Thompson's grocery store.

Camping coaches at Ravenscar
'Copyright The Francis Frith Collection'

I can remember an incident that caused me to have nightmares; four or five young calves between nine and twelve months old were mown down in the tunnel. Night after night all I could think about was this tremendous, thunderous monster ploughing into those petrified animals. The engine driver was completely unaware of the accident and continued his journey to Scarborough, but shortly afterwards, two members of the Duck family who were taking a short cut through the tunnel stumbled over the carcasses. They reported their gruesome discovery to the stationmaster who rang his Scarborough counterpart; on inspection the buffers and sides of the train were found to be splattered with blood, hair and flesh. Another distressing incident was when three dogs from separate households near Station Square disappeared one afternoon. Their whereabouts became known later in the evening when Mr Tom Lightfoot reported hearing dogs barking and sheep bleating amongst trees near the waterworks. What a pitiful sight. Several animals had been mauled and others were entangled in the barbed wire surrounding the large reservoir. When the dogs eventually returned home with wool in their teeth and blood-stained coats, it was sufficient evidence to prove their guilt, and consequently they were destroyed.

Ruins of the cement works

One property with an interesting past was the Ash Yard, which Mr White purchased in 1957. The unusual house had an arched corrugated tin roof covered with six inches of mortar; the materials used were from the nearby cement works. This small business was run by Walter Hodgson and Ted Duck, the ruins still remain today in a field adjacent to the cliff top radar station and coastguard outlook. At one time this dwelling was known as the 'Silver Fox Farm' and the pens used for housing the foxes were still intact. Years ago there had been a railway siding, which was laid for the purpose of transporting household refuse from Scarborough. The rubbish dump unfortunately attracted people collecting old bottles and jars; eventually they became a nuisance because after several months of digging large holes, the field looked more like a bomb site. To avoid being caught they returned well into the night, parked their cars in Station Square and walked down the line to their bounty!

Around 1957 my father had an interesting visit from Frank Roberts who proudly introduced the 'Fi-Cord', in other words, a portable reel-to-reel tape recorder. What fascinated me was the drawing of a small mouth and ear on the facia of the machine to indicate to other nationalities where to place the microphone and headphones.

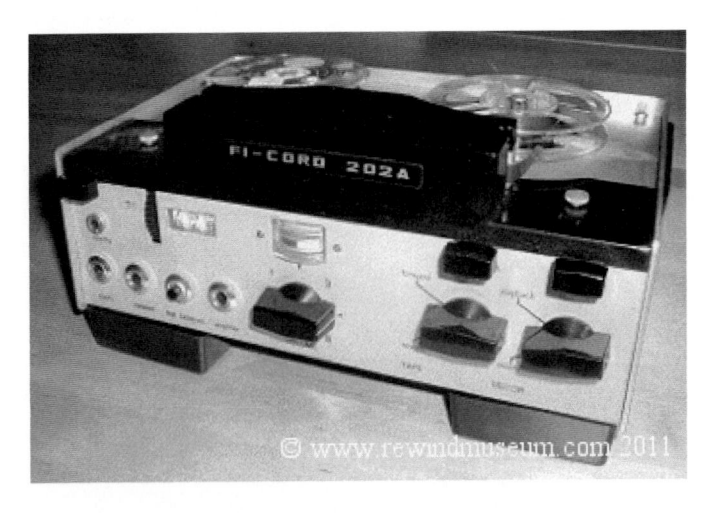

The Fi- Cord - 'Copyright The Rewind Museum.com'

A few days later he travelled to Switzerland with his invention. Although I believe Mr Roberts was the brains behind this masterpiece, it was produced by his employer, Erskine Laboratories. It was later adopted by such people as Alan Wicker on his travel documentaries.

Sunday friendly cricket matches were very popular, the hotel team was picked by the host in charge of entertainments. A familiar face in the game, who came with his family on holiday to Raven Hall, was none other than the retired Yorkshire County Cricket Club captain, Brian Sellers. Although never appearing at the crease, he was known to give advice to promising young players. Another celebrity, Eddie Waring, chose to have a getaway break at Ravenscar. He was well loved by the public for his rugby league commentaries on BBC television, and he did actually play for the opposition, much to the delight of the players and spectators.

Harry Robinson preparing the pitch for the next match

The thirtieth anniversary of the Women's Institute

The Women's Institute arranged a social gathering to celebrate their 30th anniversary on October 8th 1958. The ladies, including myself, sat down to a splendid spread of homemade fare and enjoyed the company of some founder members. Mrs Steele, our President for seven years, baked a delicious fruit cake for the occasion, which was iced and adorned with thirty lit candles.

All tenants of the Ravenscar Estate were sent a letter dated March 23rd 1959 from Maddox, Petters and Co., signed by the senior partner W.H.D. Campbell in his capacity as receiver for the company. The notification stated that rents were being revised as they had remained unchanged for many years. The higher rentals would take effect immediately; this transpired to be a fifty per cent increase.

The Home Office purchased a piece of land near the beacon top which previously sited one of the Second World War radar stations. The purpose was to build a radio mast in conjunction with another two: one at Sutton Bank near Thirsk, the other at Boulby above Staithes. These three would serve the North Riding Police Force and also the fire and ambulance services. They made use of the same eleven-thousand volt electricity cable that ran from School Lane to the beacon and had previously been installed for the R.A.F.

Whilst out horse riding on a fine summer's day in Staintondale, a Cadillac pulled up alongside me; the black-haired, slick young man at the wheel enquired if he could borrow the thoroughbred. I declined as 'Floral Mee' was only on loan from a school friend. He followed by asking "Do you know of anyone else in the area who would lend me one?" Again I couldn't help him. It was only after he drove away towards Cloughton that I realised the stranger was the popular singer Michael Holliday, who was staying at Cloughton Newlands during his summer season at the Floral Hall Theatre. His most successful hit was 'The Story of My Life'

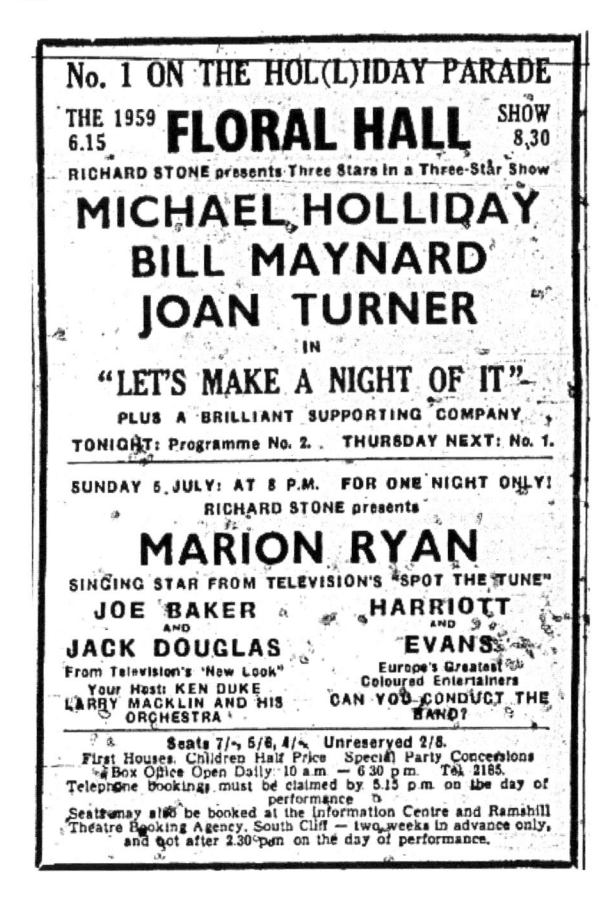

Above:
Michael Holliday

Left:
Michael Holliday advertisement for the Floral Hall in 1959

***

CHAPTER NINE

HIDDEN DANGERS

In the early sixties, signs of modernisation were evident in all aspects of village life. The daily rail service was now totally dieselised; everyone hoped these new locomotives would be as reliable as the steam engines when faced with inclement winter conditions. At the farmhouse we now had the luxury of a new bathroom complete with W.C.; no more having to sit in a tin bath in front of the coal fire and no more trips to the cold and sometimes freezing outside lavatory! Many properties supported strange looking 'H' shaped television aerials; a new telephone cable was laid on School Lane connecting the whole village to Cloughton exchange. In the church a new organ had replaced the old Binns pipe instrument, which had become riddled with woodworm. This had been a gift to the church by Sydney Carter in 1914 and was sadly broken up. Recently Mr Lancaster, his nephew, remarked *'Hadn't anyone heard of Rentokil?'*.

Shire horses were retired from all duties, combine harvesters had made the binder and threshing machine almost obsolete, and days of milking stools were now numbered with the arrival of milking machines. Occasionally, if there was a power cut, one had to revert to the old methods, and likewise Tilley lamps were retained for emergencies. With the invention of bailers, haycocks had disappeared from the fields, also there was no need to manually spread manure as a mechanical spreader did the job. Annual tuberculosis tests became compulsory in dairy herds and sheep had to be dipped.

The last threshing day

10 o'clock tea break

The stretch of land one hundred yards south of the vicarage boasted an abundance of nature with its rich carpet of wild flowers; stonecrops, pignuts, ox-eye daisies, clover, spotted orchids, scrumptious wild strawberries, bird's eye trefoils, and a wealth of purple vetch that attracted numerous spotted burnets and common blue butterflies. On the old Marine Esplanade a small area was covered with the distinctive quaking grass, which when dried was widely used in flower arranging. These meadows were also popular with skylarks, easily recognisable rising vertically from the ground and hovering overhead in song. Between this tranquil place and Raven Hall, the nuns from Cliff House could frequently be seen kneeling in prayer. When their peace was disturbed by farm workers, they immediately blessed them and prayed for their crops. Another favourite haunt was a long seat in a precarious position placed right on the cliff edge with nothing between them and the wide expanse of the North Sea. During their relaxation period and obviously in a mischievous mood, the nuns were spotted climbing the rocket post!

"You can see for miles up here!"

Mr J.R. Cooper decided it was time to retire in 1960 and sold Raven Hall to Mr Gridley. Three years later he disposed of the cricket field to Mr Goodall of Springfield Farm. Mr Cooper always gave his full support to the Men's Club and the cricket team; he also served on numerous committees. He joined Scarborough Rural District Council, and for two terms was chairman of the water and sewerage department, before it was transferred to Scarborough Corporation. Since his retirement he resided in Scarborough until his death.

Meanwhile back in Ravenscar, water meters were introduced and became compulsory at all properties that operated as a business. A small brick building in the reservoir field belonging to Church Farm housed an abandoned drip-feed chlorinator that used to be topped up daily by George Duck. About one hundred yards away, a second building that covered a very deep bore hole, also had an electricity supply connected. The long shallow reservoir was crumbling and usually in the bottom, just a few puddles of water and vegetation provided the habitat for many newts.

Shire horse 'Metal' on duty at the bore hole

However, the adjacent deep one was a dangerous place. Even with a barbed-wire surround, one young heifer managed to fall in and drown and to make matters worse, the next day it was discovered that a fox had been on a killing spree and had mutilated many hens, in fact he hadn't been satisfied until they were all dead!

Shallow reservoir

One winter's evening a hurricane force wind battered the village with such ferocity that it blew a haystack and a straw stack completely over. Astonishingly, a shed was uprooted with its three-foot anchoring posts that were set in concrete. Many properties suffered damage and large quantities of slates and tiles were being ripped off the roofs.

This also proved to be a very busy time for Ravenscar coastguards. On a warm sunny day in May, a party of schoolboys and masters came by train and decided to walk to Robin Hood's Bay. Whilst making their way down to the shore, three boys fell and a fourth got into difficulties. Police, ambulance men and coastguards had the task of carrying three stretchers up to the golf course where an ambulance was waiting. Tragically, one boy died a few days later.

A casualty of the storm

Sketch of a 'Plesiosaur'

Another adventurous group of students hit the jackpot and the Whitby Gazette reported the exciting find.

'They discovered the intact remains of a Plesiosaur, about 20 feet in length. Dr.F.M. Broadhurst, tutor in charge of the course, said that the Plesiosaur, a reptile which lived just short of two hundred million years ago, had been found in the Lias rocks at the foot of the cliffs near Ravenscar between Peak Point and Blea Wyke.' This long-necked carnivorous, marine reptile had paddle like limbs and could grow up to thirty-six feet long.

Following three weeks of dry weather, one Tuesday in early June, a fire broke out in Fox Cliff below the vicarage; with the vegetation dry as a tinder box this could have been catastrophic for the fauna and flora. The cause of the inferno was unexplained but it was exacerbated by the rapid explosions of tracer bullets, which had been discarded after the war and were shooting out in all directions. Onlookers had to be kept well away from the cliff edge for their own safety.

Little had changed in the social life of the village. The Women's Institute and Men's Club were ticking over and the cricket team was still struggling to win matches. The annual trip to Scarborough's Open Air Theatre was always welcome, but whist drives and dances had dwindled to two or three a year, and folk dancing, which once was at competition level, came to an end. When Mr and Mrs Simmons moved to Station Square, Mrs Simmons soon introduced bingo drives to raise money for the village hall. This new attraction proved to be an outstanding success and the hall was always packed. This was also a time when some well-known names left. Mr Shippey retired to live near his son in Whitby and Mr and Mrs Steele, long standing stalwarts of social life also moved away. Quite a few new people took up residence including Mr and Mrs Whitlam who lived at Crag Hill and ran a cafe from their front room serving afternoon teas. They also sold sweets, tobacco and ice cream from an alcove in the hallway. Mr Whitlam had an unusual hobby. He bred canaries and loved to show them off to friends and neighbours who were entertained by the delightful feathered songsters! Mr and Mrs Whitfield acquired Pollard Cafe next door. In Station Square Mr and Mrs Broadhead took over the post office whilst next door the village store was now run by Miss Cambage and her uncle.

Drifting snow at the chlorinator building

The Ferguson tractor passing the road to Bell Hill

Nice to see a bus at last!

"There's a haystack under here somewhere!"

The winter of 1963 had all the hallmarks of another 1947. On New Year's Day there was still a covering of snow left over from a treacherous Christmas week. Daily showers followed and by mid-January the severity of the weather increased with high winds causing deep drifts. The snow plough battled all day to keep the main route to the village open; despite many attempts Ravenscar was cut off by road for three days. The bus service from Scarborough terminated five miles away at Cloughton, however the trains continued to run. Although on one occasion a steam engine equipped with snow plough was sent to check that the line to Whitby was clear before a diesel locomotive was brought into service.

The Rev. Powell with the snowplough

Sheep in the fields were completely buried in deep snow. Usually they were found huddled together sheltering behind a wall, and their position could be spotted by giveaway signs such as small holes in the snow created by the flock's warm breath. After spending several hours carefully digging, all the sheep survived their ordeal. A very different story, however, was reported from Dartmoor where one hundred sheep were sadly found frozen to death while standing up. The residents welcomed a slow thaw but a week later, with the combination of blizzards and extremely strong winds, the road was blocked once again and bus services cancelled. A bulldozer worked all day clearing snow between the church and the mill and this cycle of events with frosty winter conditions continued until the end of February.

A curtain of ice at Tan Beck waterfall

A decision was made to demolish the derelict brickworks. It had become an unsafe playground for local teenagers, and was an area I always described as an ugly scar on the cheek of a beautiful landscape. On Sunday morning April 7th a small group of people gathered in the lane below Crag Hill, watching patiently as the Royal Engineers Territorial Army from Darlington laid explosive charges. Just before lunch the kiln went up in a cloud of dust and it was later that afternoon, when the chimneys were detonated, a few remaining spectators were rewarded with a unique experience. The ninety-foot chimney toppled over, but the smaller one appeared to disintegrate from the base. Scarborough Evening News gave a vivid description:

'It was launched just like a rocket from a pad. Smoke blasted out from underneath and out of the top, and with a roar it shot vertically into the air. As it crashed back to the ground it broke up and all the bricks landed in quite a small area.'

The Brickworks chimneys intact

'Blast off' captured by the Evening News

Mrs Powell, the vicar's wife was out having an afternoon stroll with her dog, and decided to walk along a track that had been a section of the undercliff gardens. Somehow she accidentally slipped and fell down the cliff side, but fortunately her cries for help were eventually heard by another walker. The coastguards and police took great care over the hazardous rock face to reach the injured lady, and after making her as comfortable as possible, she was stretchered back to the main path. An advance team removed tree branches overhanging the track, otherwise it would have been impossible to manoeuvre the sharp bends as they struggled up the incline in poor light. Finally, they made it to the top where the waiting ambulance took Mrs Powell to hospital. Today this pathway is completely overgrown and inaccessible.

In these remote areas, coastguards were indispensable, however during one rocket practice things didn't go according to plan. When assembling the equipment they failed to notice that the rope attaching the rocket to the hawser was frayed, because mice had chewed their way partly through it. As the coastguard fired the rocket, the 'missile' broke free and took off, out of control, with the trailing rope wrapping round an electricity mains wire causing a big flash. It was a saving grace that the rocket was stopped in its tracks before it hurtled into Station Square!

Our sure-footed coastguards who knew every safe path in the cliff were called out again with other emergency services that relied on the locals' knowledge of the terrain. On the afternoon of October 19th 1965, a party of boys and teachers who were staying at Boggle Hole Youth Hostel were looking for anything of geological interest. They were a few yards south of Blea Wyke when one boy slipped and fell several feet to the rocks. The coastguards assisted the police and ambulance crews, but it was some time before they located the youngster as there was uncertainty of his whereabouts. Once found, he was strapped to a stretcher and six men had the gruelling task of carrying the unfortunate youth up to the undercliff. A few rescuers carried Tilley lamps to illuminate the way. Police cars were parked near the vicarage with headlights on full beam to light up the cliff face and enable the brave helicopter pilot to winch him up safely.

With hopes of discovering oil and gas in the North Sea, a rig was established two miles from Ravenscar's coast. On one occasion it was reported that due to very stormy weather, the rig could have been in trouble. Local coastguards were summoned to the cliff top in case a helicopter required a suitable landing area. The wind speed recorded was 103 m.p.h. and as a result Whitby lifeboat failed to leave the harbour, but Scarborough lifeboat put to sea successfully and kept watch on the rig for twelve hours. When she arrived the coastguards returned to their beds. An article in the Evening News the following day, quoted the radio operator: *'We are taking a pounding and the rig is shaking. Conditions remain the same as before. We are in no great difficulty at the moment'*.

It was later confirmed that the only damage sustained was to the surround of the helicopter landing pad.

One of the last trains to leave Ravenscar

Double-headed steam excursion train

The last train spotters

Ravenscar lost a reliable mode of transport on March 6th 1965 when Dr. Beeching's plan to close many unprofitable railway lines was implemented. Throughout its lifetime the train played a vital part in rural journeys. For some children it was a means of getting to and from school, and it was a necessary link when visiting loved ones. The railway was also important to the tourist trade; during those days eight diesel locomotives came through Ravenscar, four from either direction. The last day drew a spectacle of onlookers, along with passengers taking a final nostalgic trip. In addition to the normal service, a double-headed steam excursion train rolled into the station. The final curtain came down as the evening diesel to Whitby arrived at eight thirty. Two and a half years later in October 1967, my father's cousin drove the very last train on the now derelict Scarborough to Whitby line. On board were some potential buyers of any removable items such as waiting rooms, platforms and wrought iron seats, but one small piece of memorabilia had mysteriously disappeared overnight – the Ravenscar station clock!

End of the line

The following year contractors moved in to dismantle the rail track and sleepers. Firstly the rails were removed and cut into manageable lengths, placed into small heaps and lifted into a large truck by a metal crane equipped with an electromagnet. It was rumoured they were recycled into razor blades. A second group came along with a powerful diesel saw and removed the sleepers, which were supposedly sent to the North East to be used as pit props in the coal mines. The men collected milk from Church Farm every day until their work was completed.

The waiting room

The waiting room becomes a cricket pavilion
Left to right: Alan & Harry Robinson, John Ward

Enter a businessman from Scalby who bought the stone from the platform at Whitaker's siding to build a bungalow for himself. Ravenscar's waiting room and wooden platform were purchased by Barry Breckon who generously gave the building to Ravenscar Cricket Club to use as its pavilion.

On June 27th, 1965 the Reverend Powell took his last service at St. Hilda's, and this was a notable event, as from that day there would no longer be a resident vicar in Ravenscar. The vicarage was sold and became a private residence known as Ness Hall. The congregation of Ravenscar, Staintondale, and Howdale became part of the flock cared for by Reverend Tubbs who was the vicar of Scalby. Three years later he was inducted at St Hilda's Church.

Following a week of heavy snow showers and frosty nights, on Saturday November 27th 1965 amidst blizzards and in poor visibility, the freighter 'Fred Everard' was in deep trouble between Raven Hall and Blea Wyke, at exactly the same spot where fifty-two years earlier the 'Coronation' had succumbed to the elements. In the early hours this cargo ship, which was carrying paper pulp from Norway to London, sent out a Mayday message and as a result Whitby lifeboat was launched. Robin Hood's Bay and Ravenscar coastguards were also called out; the telephone rang at Church Farm disturbing the whole household at 2.30am. Mary Robinson answered the call and woke Alan and Harry. Aware of the inclement weather conditions she decided to warm the cockles of their hearts by adding a tot of whisky to two mugs of tea. Along with others they made their way to the cliff top and were joined by a team from Robin Hood's Bay who had driven over the moors in appalling weather. The lifeboat arrived within ten minutes and successfully rescued the crew of fourteen after which the coastguards were immediately stood down. Eventually they arrived home at 6.00 a.m. after checking that the members from Bay had made it safely back to the Whitby road.

The Fred Everard viewed from the cliff

The sinking ship captured by the Scarborough Evening News

Three locals watch her sink!

The remains of the 'forecastle'

The drama was reported in the Scarborough Evening News on Saturday complete with photograph, consequently the next day hundreds of cars descended on the village in bright sunshine despite the treacherous roads. The situation became so serious, that for the first time ever, Ravenscar had a policeman on point duty directing traffic at the junction of Station Road and Raven Hall Road. Monday and Tuesday saw the return of squally showers and gale force winds which battered the ill-fated vessel and the forecastle was sliced from the ship's forward deck leaving the remains of a toilet in full view. Within a fortnight this came to rest at the foot of the cliff as a mangled piece of rusty metal. At one stage before she broke up, locals witnessed a large fountain of water spurting from the funnel with every incoming wave.

This is not the end of the Fred Everard saga. A salvage team came to the scene, which proved to be an expensive and unsuccessful exercise. The company owner in charge of this tricky operation, whom I shall refer to as the 'Captain', started by bringing two blue Vickers Vigor crawler tractors and a grey Ferguson down to Mill Beck. One crawler went to Ness Point to do some salvage work but became stranded and was claimed by the sea. The other made its way along the shoreline to Ravenscar forcing any small rocks aside to clear a route for the Ferguson. When the 'Captain' reached the old pump house below Raven Hall golf course he created a space in the cliff side as a park for the tractor and crawler, but it took just one rough sea to wash the Ferguson back on to the rocks causing its demise. In order to protect the Vigor he moved it to a place of safety. In the meantime, metal hawsers were thrown over the cliff above the wreck, but yet again luck was against him and they dropped on to a ledge. Undeterred he used a grappling hook and abseiled down the cliff face in order to free them, and they duly fell in place to the rocks below. The intention was to fasten the hawsers to the ship and the Vigor, and hopefully with the assistance of the waves, to pull the ship to the shore.

However, before this idea was implemented, the small salvage company went bankrupt. At the same time the 'Captain' was collecting scrap metal from the brickyard, but even this project wasn't trouble free, as his wagon became well and truly bogged down, and a local man with a tractor had to come to his aid.

Another person made an attempt to rescue the Vickers Vigor. Using a yellow Drott caterpillar, he made a route from the golf course to the undercliff known as the 'Coombs', continuing until he came across the abandoned blue crawler. The idea was to drive the blue Vigor up a steep incline to the golf course, but it soon became obvious that the track was too narrow as its blade caught the cliff side, tipping the vehicle over, and at a forty-five degree angle it slid back down. Now irretrievable, this became its final resting place. At the end of a string of debacles, the only survivor was the Drott, which returned to the village under its own steam! I only know of two items that survived the wreck, the cook's rolling pin and the ship's bell. The latter was kept on the bar in a local public house. A few months later, when a fishing boat came to the Fred Everard's watery grave with divers on board, it ran aground on the wreck and the inshore lifeboat was called to assist them.

The Vickers Vigor crawler tractor

The Ferguson meets its end!

The Drott caterpillar

The cook's rolling pin

On the 17th January 1967, when another ship was reported to have come aground beneath Raven Hall, two auxiliary coastguards went to all vantage points between Raven Hall and Blea Wyke. Having found no sight whatsoever of a boat, Mr Crowcroft, the retired subpostmaster, telephoned with this information. Apparently, shortly after sending a Mayday signal the trawler 'Andola' from Grimsby had managed to refloat free from the rocks.

It was all change in 1968: in a matter of four months the same number of households welcomed new residents. Mr and Mrs Crapper moved into the bungalow next to Station House, Miss Dickenson who had given children piano lessons at her home in Bay View, left the village and the new occupants were Mr and Mrs Hall. The other two changes of ownership resulted in two farms becoming private houses. Mr and Mrs Goodall decided to leave the village and the newcomers were Mr and Mrs Postlethwaite. Mr and Mrs Freeth moved into Mill Farm and that too became a private dwelling. This signalled the start of a decline in family owned farms and smallholdings. With the closure of the ganister works a few years earlier, and only a few farm labouring jobs along with hotel work, there was limited opportunity for residents and school leavers to work close to home.

The winter of 1969 was a repetition of 1963 but at times the storms were even more ferocious. Fortunately these winter conditions only had to be tolerated for a month. By mid-February, following a night of terrific winds with blizzards storming in from the east, extremely deep drifts had formed. Two snow ploughs and a J.C.B. digger were in action all day to keep the road passable from the Mill down to Raven Hall, but this was to no avail, as next morning it was totally blocked. Buses also were casualties and all services were cancelled. On the third day the plough managed to gain access by mid-afternoon. It was noticeably evident Ravenscar missed the vital rail link, as this time they were completely cut off with no alternative transport for three whole days – it was a case of a lifeline lost.

***

CHAPTER 10

A VILLAGE FOREVER

A familiar sight each May was the annual pilgrimage of the Duck Family. Lawrence, George and Tom made their way up the main road to the mill, along Moorland Road (also known as Green Lane) carrying cutting spades over their shoulders with one pushing a wheelbarrow, to their ultimate destination, the peat bogs about three miles across the moor, quite close to the Falcon Inn. The tradition of burning peat on the fire still continued in their individual homes and it had a wonderful earthy aroma albeit in a smoky atmosphere. Once cut into 'bricks' they were laid out, but unlike hay which took only a few days to dry the peat required all the summer months for this process. Finally, it was placed into small heaps ready for collection by Mr Bridge with his flat-bed wagon. These three households would have a plentiful supply stacked nearby to last them through the winter. After a few years Lawrence was left on his own and he continued to cut the peat well into his eighties. He was also known for his home brewing and took great pleasure in entertaining friends with his potent liquors.

Lawrence Duck

At Raven Hall Hotel the Gridley family were saddened by the death of Mr Gridley, after which his sons Michael and Paul took over the business and continued to improve and upgrade the hotel.

In the 1969-70 season the table tennis team was highly successful, the players were Geoff White, Tony Mitten and Alan Robinson. Not losing a match, they were promoted into the first division, but unfortunately, the following year they were unable to guarantee a team and thus Ravenscar had played its last game. The winners' shield was on display in the Shepherds Arms bar until it was returned to the league. All home games had been played in the village hall. An observant member on the hall committee realised that Johnson Robinson, now living at Cloughton, was the last surviving trustee, and as a result nominated names were put forward for his approval.

Mr and Mrs Robin Forbes and their son moved into 'Ravenheath' on August 10th 1970. Shortly afterwards a handful of private school pupils began boarding at the house and they rented Raven Hill in Bent Rigg Lane to use as classrooms. This very small school started as a mere acorn in Robin Hood Road, but the search was soon extended elsewhere to find suitable premises that would lend itself to future conversions, making this small fruit grow into a large oak tree. The chosen place was Wellow House in Nottinghamshire which rapidly expanded taking many more students and Mr Forbes continued to teach there. In the world of education, Wellow House must be regarded as a tremendous success story. Some years later Mr Forbes also purchased two plots of land adjacent to his home from the Robinsons; the rough piece of land became a beautiful landscaped garden.

In the early seventies there were four incidents involving auxiliary coastguards and helicopters. The rescuers found a suitable landing place amongst the small rocks, one man would then stand with an arm raised in the air to indicate to the pilot the chosen area, and would move to safety at the last minute. The first call out was not for a cliff fall but to a diabetic youngster who became ill below the Coombs. The helicopter airlifted the patient straight to hospital. Following this, a youngster who fell a few feet on to the rocks close to Mr Shippey's 'small harbour' suffered minor injuries and was flown direct to hospital. When the helicopter had come into land, the downdraught from the blades had created a massive dust storm from the shale on the cliff face and the beret of a coastguard was whipped away never to be seen again. Another incident involving a teenager was close to Tan Beck. The ambulance became bogged down on the road to Low Peak, a tractor pulled it free and it was instructed to make its way back to the golf course. A helicopter was summoned from Northumberland, because there were none available at Leconfield, but unfortunately this recovery had a tragic outcome. The last one involved two fishermen from Robin Hood's Bay who were stranded in a coble that had been battered by strong winds on to the rocks south of Blea Wyke. After searching the sea area they were spotted by the pilot scrambling to safety, a winchman was lowered down to help them. All the rescuers, including the crewman and fishermen were guided in darkness up a rough cliff path, eventually surfacing by the coastguard lookout. After all this the waiting helicopter flew off with just the winchman!

During the final few months before Staintondale School closed, one small boy had a frightening experience when the toggle fastening of his duffle coat became trapped in the minibus door as he stepped out. He ran alongside the vehicle until his little legs couldn't carry him any further, fortunately at this moment the toggle snapped off. Next morning the driver said "impossible", but the evidence was there on the floor in front of the passenger seat. For the last twenty years Ravenscar children had been travelling to this neighbouring village, however the length of their journey was about to be doubled with the closure of the school in 1974. They had been under the guidance of Miss Outhet and no doubt would also miss the wholesome hot lunches served in the village hall by Mrs Ward. Transport was arranged in the form of a school bus to the newly opened Lindhead School at Burniston where the headmistress, Miss B. Foord was joined by the familiar face of Miss Outhet.

A surprise planning application suddenly appeared in the local press requesting permission to build on twenty one plots at Ravenscar. This was submitted by a descendant of the original purchaser, but as they had not been fenced in at the time of purchase, he had no legal claim to the land.

The passing of Miss Martha Jackson in 1975, often referred to by her nickname 'Nellie', gives me the opportunity to shine some light on this remarkable lady, who was often the subject of unkind remarks regarding her unkempt appearance because later in life she suffered from facial hair growth. Miss Jackson was the custodian of the village hall key and I remember in the depth of winter having to collect it when father was putting tables and chairs in place for a whist drive. I tapped on the door before entering into a dingy room where a lone figure was sitting in the corner with a small paraffin lamp for light and the glow from a few coals being the only source of heat. Her only companions were a dozen hens in the kitchen who didn't take kindly to strangers in their home; they would flap around, flying on to the table or sideboard. My grandparents and parents gave her the respect she deserved and to them this lady was always addressed as Miss Jackson who had served the community well. She was remembered for assisting her parents in the post office and delivering the mail come rain, hail, or snow.

In due course she moved across the road to Moorcroft, where she remained for the rest of her life. Miss Jackson was a staunch supporter of the church and was responsible for lighting the coke stoves in the village hall, making certain there was always a warm welcome. When it became too painful to walk there, she was seen on more than one occasion crawling on hands and knees the short distance rather than letting the public down. What dedication! When the property became vacant, although needing complete modernisation, it was an attractive buy because of the adjacent small paddock and old stables, which once had been home to the ganister horses.

A young Miss Martha Jackson

One retired farm worker treated himself to an automatic washing machine. He carefully loaded all the clothes in, but struggled to get them out. A friend called to see how he was getting on with the new gadget, his reply was "'twas wus th'n lambin' an awd yow"!

Two once-in-a-lifetime experiences happened as a result of powerful easterlies, gusting to extreme levels and both involved the outfall sewers. From time to time when working near the rocket post one could feel a fine mist falling on to the skin. I can categorically say this was not due to the incoming tide but was the spray from the outfall pipe. One day sewerage was seen spurting forth from the cliff edge and rising vertically to about seventy feet as it was blown inland towards Station Road. Eighteen months later, when the temperature was several degrees below freezing, it was impossible to walk, let alone work in the field above the second outfall. The land was covered in a lumpy, frozen deposit, as the raw excrement blew inland and froze on impact with the ground.

Frozen 'poo'!

The cricket team was enjoying their usual Saturday afternoon match when a glider appeared. Conditions were breezy and the pilot, obviously concerned about the proximity of the sea, realised the players were not going to leave the pitch so had to make an emergency landing in the outfield. The next day it was dismantled and taken away by truck back to Sutton Bank, its launching point. About the same time during a Round Britain Microlight Race, one participant came down in bad visibility, landing in Mr Goodall's field. He stayed for two hours until the fog lifted before taking off to continue the race.

In 1975, Scarborough Borough Council purchased the track bed of the old railway line and included in the deal were the various stone-built stations. It became a new public pathway that continues to be enjoyed by walkers, cyclists and horse riders. The local riding school in Crag Lane and the trekking centre at Peak Side appreciated this new route. Within a short time the Parent Teachers' Association of the new school decided to arrange a sponsored walk from Ravenscar to Cloughton, and the sun shone brightly on these excited youngsters striding out, as was captured by the Scarborough Evening News photographer.

School children stepping out on the sponsored walk

Frank Roberts and his family left the village and headed to the North East, where he joined Victor Products of Wallsend. His knowledge of electronics led him to spearhead another invention and in 1976 the company was granted the Queen's Award for Technological Achievement in the development of 'Intrinsically Safe Coal

Face Lighting'. Although part of a team, it was acknowledged that it was Frank's ingenuity that had won the award. Mr Roberts later travelled to Buckingham Palace to be presented with the award by Her Majesty the Queen.

The church bazaar, which had been successfully held in August for many years had to continue as a summer Fair as the vicar had banned all church fundraising events and started up a planned giving scheme. We were now issued with small brown envelopes in which to place our collection money for the offertory plate.

Robin Hood's Bay had a poor television signal and the residents were delighted with news that this was about to change. In 1977 the Home Office decided to replace the existing mast at Ravenscar and purchased some extra land in the beacon field belonging to Church Farm. The BBC paid for the erection of a new one, which would eventually also have the emergency service aerials attached. Several months later a decision was made to replace the old electricity supply cable for safety reasons.

A rare picture of the old and new, side by side

The Women's Institute led by Miss Brewer arranged to plant two cherry trees alongside the village hall, one to mark the Queen's silver jubilee and the other to celebrate their own forthcoming golden anniversary.

Mr and Mrs Coultas retired from the post office in Station Square and the business transferred to new premises at Pollard Cafe. The telephone box was also moved to Church Corner and I am sure the ever increasing numbers of 'Lyke Wake' walkers would have been very grateful for this amenity at the end of their forty-mile trek from Osmotherly, a few miles east of Northallerton. However, in Ravenscar toilet facilities were sadly lacking, and there were two canvas gazebos on the edge of the cricket field followed by much more efficient portable loos, situated adjacent to Church Farm. Eventually there was the welcome arrival of a modern toilet block in Raven Hall Road. Around this time all the rough surface was removed from Station Road and used as hardcore for the new lay-by, thereby allowing visitors to park and admire the beautiful expanse of the bay. Of course the work didn't stop there, as Raven Hall and Station roads were re-laid with 'Tarmac'.

Cutting through the huge snow drifts

As my story draws to a close it would not be Ravenscar without the inclusion of another memorable winter. In mid-March 1979 the north of England was gripped by atrocious weather very similar to that of 1947, but only lasting for two weeks. At Ravenscar and surrounding areas the snowploughs were battling to prevent wind-blown snow from blocking the roads and many motorists were stranded on the Whitby road including myself at Wragby. I remember standing in the barn all morning just waiting for the storm to abate, but it never did. I trudged to the main road, the snow almost to the top of my wellingtons, where the police were helping to free vehicles one by one. After a while they organised a lift for me with another lady motorist.

With gale force winds and continuous blizzards the electricity supply was cut off between Cloughton and Ravenscar and the following day the snowdrifts were several feet deep. After thirty six hours the North Eastern Electricity Board's 'Snowcat' bulldozer made it to Staintondale and the workmen reconnected the power supply. Unfortunately the caterpillar needed some emergency repairs before it could continue its journey and these were carried out by a local agricultural engineer. Some properties were not illuminated until ten o'clock in the evening after two full days without electricity, but it was the following morning before power was restored to the whole village. A spokesman for the NEEB explained: *"When conductors crash together they short circuit..........if this continues to happen or the conductors stay stuck together, it will blow a fuse."* The farmers had to revert back to the traditional way of milking bringing their three legged stools and milk buckets out of retirement, for two days several gallons of milk were wasted when it was impossible for the tanker to get through. There was a limit to the amount of milk puddings that could be consumed! Others were struggling in the lambing sheds without lights and had to use Tilley lamps, but we were fortunate as our lambs were not due until the first week in April.

After being without wheels for four days the road conditions improved sufficiently for me to retrieve my vehicle with the aid of a tractor. The old post box was also a casualty when deep snowdrifts formed at the junction of Church Road and Raven Hall Road and snow completely filled the inside. Consequently the postman had to cover the aperture with a hessian sack to prevent any post being sent.

The vulnerable postbox

In farming things didn't always go to plan and on one day a group of youths staying at Cliff House created mischief by unravelling the hay bales, causing extra work at a very busy time. Needless to say, the baler had to be taken back to the field. The farm continued to upgrade its machinery and the six-foot cut combine harvester was replaced with an eight-foot six-inch one. The Ministry of Health and Safety made annual farm visits to check that protective guards were fitted to all machinery. On one of these visits they saw a small child and strongly advised that the pond should be filled in. Instantly, dozens of frogs were robbed of their breeding habitat and the deep contented croaks heard in the mating season, which filled the stillness of the night, were gone.

Combine harvester

An annual circular to all landowners from the Department of the Environment stipulated that they should not plough any field which was the site of an ancient barrow. Many decades before, one in the beacon field had been excavated, but nothing was found. The National Trust purchased the site of the old Alum Works plus a large stretch of land along the cliff top, taking in the fields surrounding the Marine Esplanade. New trees were planted near Station Road just before the Coastguard premises on what was formally two tennis courts with solid cinder bases. These had been built on unsold plots before new ones were laid next to the village hall during the 1920s.

Jim Robinson had decided to retire from farming at Wragby and to move back across the moor to his birthplace. The ideal smallholding, 'Sunny Hill', was available where he could continue to keep a few sheep, goats and ponies. Shortly afterwards a Scarborough man sold him a four-acre field opposite St. Hilda's Church which he used for haymaking to supplement the winter fodder. Later on, Jim wanted to give something back to the village. This field would make a permanent home for Ravenscar Cricket Club and so it was transferred into the names of chosen trustees, himself included.

There were signs of a decline in local farming. In contrast, the tourist industry was expanding, encouraged by the National Trust visitors' centre and local tea rooms. There were many interesting heritage walks to explore including a visit to the 'Two Sisters', a pair of unusual rock formations. Ravenscar became a magnet for visitors and for the colony of seals whose numbers have multiplied. They can often be seen on the rocks below Raven Hall.

"*I see no ships!*"

Visitor at one of the Two Sisters

Church Farm, which had served three generations of Robinsons stretching back to 1913, was sold to Mr and Mrs Williams in 1982. Everything comes to an end and life moves on, so now it seems to be an appropriate time to bring my story to a close. However, it always gives me great pleasure to re-visit this very beautiful village and to remember the many happy years I lived there, never forgetting some of the people who moulded Ravenscar into what it has become today.

Farewell

***

APPENDIX

VISIBLE SIGNS TODAY OF OLD RAVENSCAR

Above: Hammond Road
Below: Original manhole cover

Above: Mound of grass now covering the base of the middle shelter
Below: Base of shelter near Raven Hall

Above: A Ravenscar brick
Below: Part of the brickwork kiln

Above: Railway bridge near the brickworks
Below: Entrance to the railway tunnel

Refuge opening inside the tunnel

The station platform in spring

****